THEMED LESSON PLANS

for

RIDING INSTRUCTORS

THEMED LESSON PLANS

for

RIDING INSTRUCTORS

A Handbook for Teaching Recreational Riders

MELISSA TROUP BA, BHSII

KENILWORTH PRESS

First published in the UK in 2006 by
Kenilworth Press, an imprint of Quiller Publishing Ltd

British Library Cataloguing in Publication Data
A catalogue record for this book is available from the British Library.

ISBN 1-872119-89-1
    978-1-872119-89-2

Layout and typesetting by Kenilworth Press
Diagrams by Michael J. Stevens
Main cover illustration by Dianne Breeze

Printed and bound in Great Britain by Biddles (www.biddles.co.uk)

KENILWORTH PRESS
An imprint of Quiller Publishing Ltd
Wykey House, Wykey, Shrewsbury, SY4 1JA
tel: 01939 261616 fax: 01939 261606
e-mail: info@quillerbooks.com
website: www.kenilworthpress.co.uk

CONTENTS

ACKNOWLEDGEMENTS

I would like to thank all the staff at Liege Manor Equestrian Centre, Vale of Glamorgan, for their support and encouragement.

I would like to pay special thanks to Sarah Bassett BHSI – without your exceptional training and support, I would not be in the position to have written the book.

Thanks are also due to Michael Stevens for converting my lesson plan roughs into such clear diagrams, and to British Dressage for permission to reproduce the dressage tests in Chapter 11.

MELISSA TROUP

AUTHOR'S NOTE

As an instructor it takes time to build up a repertoire of exercises to suit all ages and abilities. This book provides a wide range of themed lesson plans, with notes on how these can be adapted and developed for the different levels of recreational rider, from beginner to advanced, whether children or adults.

Each riding school uses its own system of grading riders, and instructors must assess each rider, or group of riders and decide which level of lesson plan they feel would be most suitable.

Remember that not all riders may have a comprehensive basic grounding in their work. You may assess a rider who has ridden for many years, but, for example, has never been introduced to lateral work. In this instance, the rider may be very competent, but the lateral work would need to be introduced from beginner level.

LESSON PLANS

The lesson plans in this book are organised into themes (teaching subjects) – for example, circles, transitions, drill ride work – to allow instructors to go straight to a chosen topic and find exercises to suit riders of different abilities.

Each exercise includes the following:

- rider level – this is a guide for the level of rider that the exercise is aimed at;

- aims and benefits – at the beginning of each chapter there is a list of generic aims and benefits for the theme; specific aims and benefits are listed with the exercise;

- exercise – a detailed lesson plan, which develops in difficulty according to rider ability;

- problems – the problems are specific to the exercise and may refer to riders and/or horses.

The exercises are mainly designed for use in one-hour group lessons, teaching one or more exercises during the hour, as required. They can be adapted for half-hour group and private lessons.

The book assumes the use of a 20m x 40m arena, but each exercise can be adapted for a differently sized school.

> NB: Some exercises, for example circles in canter, appear twice – in the chapter on circles and again in the chapter on canter. This has been done for ease of use, enabling instructors to locate exercises on particular themes in one section.

1 CLASSIFICATION OF RIDER ABILITY

In this book, the terms **beginner**, **novice**, **intermediate** and **advanced** are used in relation to recreational riders. These terms should not be confused with the grading systems used for competitive riders in dressage, show-jumping and eventing.

TINY TOTS

Many riding schools offer half-hour group lessons for young children (four- to six-year-olds). Most will be lead-rein lessons. However, if they start riding at four, and need to remain in half-hour lessons for reasons of physical development only, they will probably be relatively competent by six years old, having ridden for two years, and may even have started cantering with or without leaders. Some of the exercises can be condensed or changed slightly for this younger age group.

BEGINNER

Riders are classified as beginners from their first riding lesson until they are confident and able to walk and trot unaided, on an accommodating horse or pony, while going large and on 20m circles. They should be able to control their horse in walk and trot, maintaining a distance of one horse's length between themselves and the rider in front. They should be developing balance in their position.

NOVICE

Novice riders develop their work in walk and trot, to include:

- riding further school figures;

- understanding the reasons for riding on the correct diagonal (younger children may not be able to recognise the 'correct' diagonal until later, but they should be able to change their diagonal when asked);

- starting to work without stirrups or reins to improve position, suppleness, confidence and balance;

- riding a variety of changes of rein;

- starting to develop the ability to ride smooth, progressive upwards and downwards transitions;

- beginning to work in jumping position, and starting to work over poles and possibly small fences as they progress.

Novice riders will be introduced to canter, building their ability until they can apply the correct aids for the transition themselves, maintaining control in the canter during simple exercises.

They should understand and start to maintain a correct basic position during all three paces. They should be encouraged to develop 'feel' early on and develop co-ordination of the aids.

There will be a difference in the understanding of theory between children and adults. Children will learn the theory through following instructions, trial and error and acting instinctively. Adults enjoy understanding a concept and have the ability to do so.

INTERMEDIATE

The intermediate rider will be further developing the work carried out at novice level. New work to introduce will include:

- direct transitions,

- shortening and lengthening of the stride,

- basic lateral work – leg yielding and turn on the forehand.

The basic position should be more established, developing a deeper seat and security of the lower leg, allowing more effective application of the aids.

The jumping position should also develop security and riders should be able to maintain the rhythm while riding simple jumping exercises, keeping their balance as they jump, so that they do not interfere with the horse.

The rider should begin to develop `feel' for the horse's correct way of going. In the beginning this may only be a glimmer, but the rider should `feel' when it is correct through instruction.

ADVANCED

Again, advanced riders develop from the previous stages, further improving security in their positions – both the basic position and the jumping position, which will lead to greater effectiveness of the aids and therefore greater influence of the horse.

The advanced rider should be able to improve the horse's way of going by having a greater understanding of when and why the quality may be lost and, in that knowledge, work to prevent the loss by riding positively for what they want.

A good advanced rider should be able to ride a preliminary or easy novice dressage test well, and be able to ride a quality round of a 70cm (2ft 3in) show-jumping course, at home, on a horse that they know well.

2 FIRST AND EARLY LESSONS

Initial lessons offer the rider the opportunity to try a new hobby or sport. For the rider to want to continue, certain criteria must be met at each lesson:

- the lesson must be professional and well structured,

- a suitable horse or pony must be allocated,

- the rider must enjoy the lesson,

- progress must be made,

- confidence must be developed.

Riders are often offered a variety of choices for their initial lessons:

- on the lunge,

- private lessons,

- in a group, beginners together.

Instructors will be able to advise prospective clients which lesson is thought to be the most suitable. When booking the first lesson the new rider should be given advice about suitability of clothing.

THE FIRST LESSON

AIMS FOR THE FIRST LESSON

1. WELCOME AND MOUNTING

A warm welcome
A smile, and an introduction to the instructor and horse or pony, will help to relax the rider.

Allocation of a suitable horse/pony, correctly tacked-up
Hopefully, every centre has faithful and generous 'friends' who excel at teaching beginners to ride.

Teach the rider to mount
Whether this be from the ground, a mounting block or via a leg-up.

Adjust the girth and stirrups
Talk the rider through the process. As a rough guide, a suitable stirrup length for the beginner can be assessed by setting the base of the stirrup to reach the ankle when the leg hangs straight down.

Holding the reins
Basics should be taught correctly from the start. Include how to shorten and lengthen the reins and the position of the hands.

Explain the basic position
Ear, shoulder, hip and heel should be in line, with the stirrup on the ball of the foot and the heel

slightly lower than the toe.

Starting, stopping and steering
Explain the aids.

2. INTRODUCTION TO WALKING

Early walk work
Leading or on the lunge, early walk work includes halt to walk transitions and positional encouragement. If going large, ride simple changes of rein to introduce steering.

20m circles in walk
Explain how to ride 20m circles at A and C, and practise.

3. INTRODUCTION TO TROT

Explanation while halted
Explain the difference in the beat between walk and trot. Explain sitting and rising trot. Using a neck strap, the rider can practise rising and sitting.

First trot in sitting trot
Controlling the horse, trot a short distance with the rider in sitting trot to give the feel of the pace. This can be repeated.

Rising trot
Once the rider has the feel of the trot, introduce rising for short periods. Calling out 'rise' and 'sit', or 'up' and 'down' in the horse's rhythm will help the rider to feel and find the rhythm.

EARLY LESSONS

Early lessons develop the skills learned during the first lesson, be they on the lunge or going large. When on the lunge, progress is often rapid regarding balance and position of the rider. Once these are more established, the rider can learn to control the horse off the lunge.

AIMS FOR THE EARLY LESSONS

Position
The rider often requires minor positional corrections. Correcting at this stage means that bad habits, which are harder to correct later, are not formed.

Balance and rhythm
With practice comes the rider's balance and rhythm in the trot.

Increased rider fitness
Gradual build-up of suppleness and stamina.

Confidence
Every lesson should develop confidence.

Co-ordination of the aids
An improved, balanced position will help co-ordination of the aids. If not already taught in the first lesson, the rider needs to be taught the aids for the transitions between walk and trot.

Accuracy
Ask for halt transitions at letters. Talk about preparation and communication with the horse. Make transitions from trot to walk between two letters.

CHILDREN

Coming off the lead rein.

There are many factors that affect this decision: age, ability, strength, confidence. Start to wean the child off the leader by having the leader running next to the pony, but not actually holding on. During the course of the lesson, the instructor can bring the leader into the middle of the school, replacing them if necessary.

20m circles

Develop the ability to ride 20m circles at A and C initially, progressing to 20m circles at E or B.

Trot diagonals

Often an adult will understand the theory, and recognise trot diagonals better than a child. Depending on age, it may be better to leave this subject until the child is older.

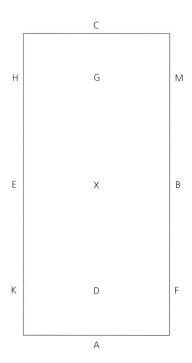

20 x 40m ARENA, WITH LETTERS

3 TRANSITIONS

The aim of a transition is to improve the horse's way of going. Good communication and preparation from the rider should ensure that the transition is smooth, balanced and harmonious.

BEGINNER

- Learn to start and stop the horse when asked – transitions are initially about control.

- Understand the natural aids – seat, legs, hands and voice, and be aware of the artificial aids – the whip and spurs.

- Maintain a good basic position during the transition. Often this is lost with the beginner rider through sheer enthusiasm to do what is asked. For example, often when using the legs, the rider will inadvertently pull on the reins. While correcting the mistake, we must be careful not to quell the enthusiasm.

- Make progressive transitions between halt, walk and trot.

- Develop 'feel' on different horses for how much leg and hand are needed to ride a smooth transition.

NOVICE

- Develop greater co-ordination of the aids.

- Ride progressive transitions on school figures, e.g. circles, maintaining the shape of the figure.

- Begin to develop 'feel' for when the basic transitions are balanced and correctly executed.

- Begin to develop a secure position, which will help the clear application of the aids.

- Start to introduce the canter transition, initially aided by the instructor, and then controlled by the rider.

INTERMEDIATE

- Develop the ability to ride balanced transitions through all three paces, including transitions within the pace.

- Start to ride direct transitions.

- Understand the theory of how to maintain balance, rhythm, impulsion, suppleness and straightness during a transition, by developing a connection between leg and hand. Start to put this theory into practice.

- Develop a lightness of the aids.

ADVANCED

- Understand the concept of the 'correct way of going' for the horse during transitions, both upwards and downwards, progressive and direct, and to include transitions within the pace. Try to achieve this by further developing 'feel'.

- Have a little understanding of which transition exercises should improve the horse, depending on the horse's natural way of going, temperament and level of training.

AIMS AND BENEFITS

RIDER

- Position – balance and security.
- Co-ordination of the aids.
- Feel.

HORSE

- Impulsion.
- Rhythm.
- Balance.
- Suppleness.
- Straightness.
- Engagement.

WALK AND TROT EXERCISES IN CLOSED ORDER

1. TRANSITION BOXES

RIDER LEVEL Tiny tots and beginner children.

AIMS AND BENEFITS
- Control in halt, walk and trot.
- Develops co-ordination, confidence and accuracy.

EXERCISES 1 AND 2
- Make two 'boxes' out of poles, on either side of the track along one long side of the school.

- Have the ride halt along the opposite long side.

EXERCISE 1

- Ask lead file in succession to make a transition from walk to halt in the box. Halt for a count of 5 horses, crocodiles, or whatever is fun, before walking on again.

EXERCISE 2

- The lead file in trot makes a transition to walk in the first box, a transition to trot in the second box, and then trots to the rear of the ride.

PROBLEMS, Exercises 1 and 2
- Lack of preparation for the transition.

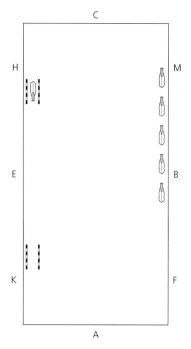

EXERCISES 1 and 2

- Loss of position due to reins being too long or too short.

- Confusing aids for the pony due to an insecure position.

- Ponies may need encouragement to return to trot once they have walked, especially if they are nearing the rear of the ride!

2. TRANSITIONS FROM THE REAR OF THE RIDE

RIDER LEVEL Tiny tots; beginner and novice riders, either as part of the warm up, or for the lesson.

AIMS AND BENEFITS

- Co-ordination, independence and accuracy.
- Practice of halt, walk and trot transitions.
- Keeping the ride moving if it is cold.
- A good exercise, especially in trot if the horses or ponies are a little fresh in winter.

EXERCISE 3

- Whole ride to go large in walk.

- Rear file in succession makes a transition to halt at a given letter or as asked by the instructor.

- Rider remains in halt until the rest of the ride has caught up, and then makes a transition to walk to become the lead file. This will require them to glance behind to observe the ride's progress.

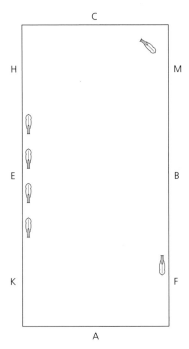

EXERCISES 3 and 4

EXERCISE 4

- The same exercise can be ridden in trot with the rear file making a transition to walk, remaining in walk until the ride has caught up, and then trotting on again.

PROBLEMS, Exercises 3 and 4

- Loss of position or balance in the transitions.
- Aids unclear.
- Riders do not always make their upward transitions at the front of the ride in time, causing the rest of the ride to make a downward transition to compensate.
- Horses or ponies not used to being at the front of the ride, because they are not natural-born leaders, can be more awkward to ride.

EXERCISE 5

- Both of these exercises can be ridden with the ride divided up onto two 20m circles. (Opposing reins on the circles are best so the horses do not meet head-on when they pass at X.)

PROBLEMS

- As for Exercises 3 and 4.
- Loss of shape of the circle.

3. MAKE TRANSITIONS AS A RIDE, MAINTAINING A DISTANCE

RIDER LEVEL Novice and intermediate.

AIMS AND BENEFITS

- Learning to prepare adequately for transitions.
- Co-ordination of aids, accuracy.
- Independence while riding transitions.

EXERCISE 6

- Ask the ride to maintain one horse's distance (easier) or one letter's distance (more difficult) between them.

- Ask the ride to make transitions, following the instructor's commands through halt, walk and trot, maintaining their distances. (Try to allow sufficient preparation time so that the riders make transitions at the letters, thus gauging and helping to keep their distances.)

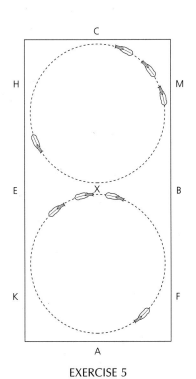

EXERCISE 5

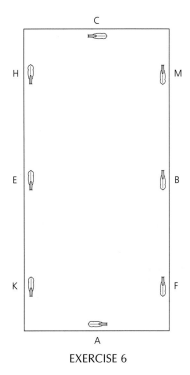

EXERCISE 6

PROBLEMS

- Riders do not maintain their distances because they are unable to assess their horse's ground-covering ability. Here you must help to push on the slower ones, and encourage the more forward thinking to contain their horse's energy.
- Lack of preparation, resulting in unbalanced transitions.
- Loss of position during the transition.
- This is a difficult exercise, but when ridden well the whole group enjoys a sense of achievement.

CANTER EXERCISES IN CLOSED ORDER

1. RIDE IN HALT, LEAD FILE CANTERS LARGE TO THE REAR OF THE RIDE

RIDER LEVEL Novices starting to canter.

AIMS AND BENEFITS

- To 'feel' the transition to canter, which is controlled by the instructor.

EXERCISE 7

- Halt the ride at E or B.

- Lead file in succession makes transitions through walk and trot to canter in an allocated corner, and continues the canter to the rear of the ride. Repeat on the other rein.

- The instructor must be in control of the canter transition and maintain the pace to the rear of the ride in order for the rider to relax into the movement.

- Explain the exercise in detail to the whole ride and encourage questions. The first canters are huge milestones for most riders and they must feel confident in what they are being asked to do.

- Explain how the rider should sit and hold the saddle in the canter, and explain the movement the horse makes and how to move with it.

PROBLEMS

- A tense position, resulting in difficulty in sitting to the canter.
- Leaning forwards in the canter, making the rider vulnerable and unbalancing the horse.

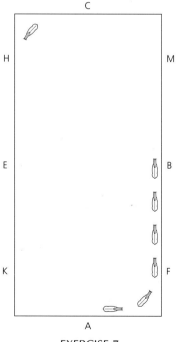

EXERCISE 7

- When teaching the novice rider to canter, it is important to use a reliable and comfortable horse with an easy, balanced and rhythmical canter that is easily controlled by the instructor.

2. RIDE IN HALT, LEAD FILE MAKES A TRANSITION TO CANTER AT X ON A 20M CIRCLE

RIDER LEVEL Novice.

AIMS AND BENEFITS

- As previous exercise, with a slightly longer canter, offering the rider more time to 'feel' and sit to the movement.
- Teaching and encouraging riders to give the aids for the transition themselves.

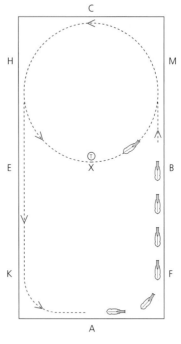

EXERCISE 8

Ⓣ = transition

EXERCISE 8

- Halt the ride at E or B.

- Lead file in succession walk and trot.

- Ride a 20m circle at A or C with a transition to canter at X.

- Continue the circle in canter and maintain the pace to the rear of the ride. Repeat on the other rein.

PROBLEMS

- Depending on the reliability of the horse or pony, you may need to ask for the canter transition after X, closer to the boards. This will ensure that the horse continues on the circle and does not change direction at X, to the opposite end of the school!

Continue using these two exercises until the rider is balanced and starting to develop the seat in canter. You can introduce and improve the rider's aids for canter using these exercises, and discuss contact on the reins in the canter and the subsequent downward transitions to trot and walk, which will offer the rider sufficient challenges so that the exercises do not become stale.

3. RIDE IN WALK, LEAD FILE IN SUCCESSION CANTERS TO THE REAR OF THE RIDE

RIDER LEVEL Novice (and intermediate warm-up).

AIMS AND BENEFITS
- Once the seat is more established, cantering large will give the rider a different sense of balance between the long sides and the corners. The canter may be affected by or affect the rider's position.

EXERCISE 9

- The ride walks large.

- Lead file in succession makes a transition to trot, allowing sufficient preparation time for a transition to canter in a named corner.

- Lead file canters to the rear of the ride preparing sufficiently for balanced transitions to trot and walk.

EXERCISE 10

- It is far safer at this level to have the ride in walk when the lead file makes the transition to canter, but the ride can safely trot in between the cantering.

- As the lead file joins the rear of the ride, ask the whole ride to 'trot on'.

- Name the corner for the next lead file to make the transition to canter and ask the rest of the ride to

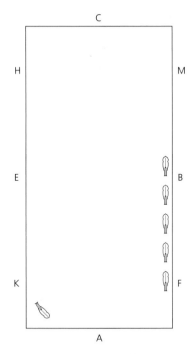

EXERCISES 9 and 10

make a downward transition to walk in the previous corner, e.g. lead file canter between A and K, the rest of the ride walk at F.

The frequency of transitions keeps the riders alert and benefits the horses' responsiveness to the aids.

PROBLEMS, Exercises 9 and 10
- The rider may find maintaining the canter for a longer period of time more difficult than earlier exercises.
- The horse may become long and flat along the long sides, and as a result may lose balance in the corners and break into trot.
- The rider may lose balance.

4. CANTER LARGE, INCLUDING A 20M CIRCLE AT THE FREE END OF THE SCHOOL

RIDER LEVEL Good novice and intermediate.

AIMS AND BENEFITS

- Developing the ability to maintain the canter for longer periods.
- Introducing a 20m circle ridden in canter.
- Planning ahead.

EXERCISE 11

- With the ride in walk, lead file makes a progressive transition into canter.

- Canter a 20m circle at the 'free' end of the school, before continuing the canter to the rear of the ride.

- Explain that the 'free' end of the school is the opposite end to the rest of the ride, e.g. if the ride is walking at the A end of the school, the lead file would canter a 20m circle at C, C being the 'free' end of the school.

PROBLEMS

- Across the different levels you will expect different levels of accuracy of the circle. The first time a novice rider rides a 20m circle in canter it may not be the perfect shape or size but should improve relatively quickly. If you have spent time initially developing riders' balance and seat in the canter, you will usually find they will pleasantly surprise you!
- Many horses will become long and flat along the long sides in the canter and may fall into trot if not corrected.

- The 20m circle usually helps to connect the canter again, partly because of the shape and partly because the circle will be the rider's focus and they will therefore ride it more strongly. Riders then often take a 'breather' having achieved the circle, which is when the horse will fall into trot. Explain this to the riders and encourage them to keep riding the canter between leg and hand at all times.

- Children do not always find it easy to decide whether they should circle at A or C. The instructor may need to control this decision.

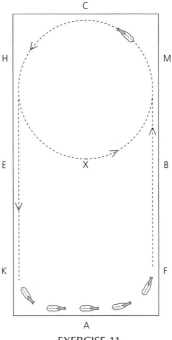

EXERCISE 11

TRANSITION EXERCISES IN OPEN ORDER

1. HALF 20M CIRCLE EXERCISES

RIDER LEVEL Novice, intermediate and advanced.

AIMS AND BENEFITS
- Working independently.
- Riding transitions while maintaining the shape of the half 20m circle.
- Using the half circle to increase engagement of the transition.
- Accuracy.

EXERCISES 12–14

- Each rider works independently on the exercise, riding a half 20m circle from anywhere along a named long side, e.g. KEH, across the school, arriving opposite the point that they left, on the other long side of the school, i.e. MBF.

- Explain that the riders already on the track have right of way over the riders joining the track from the half circle.

- The riders make transitions as they cross the centre line, on the half 20m circle.

EXERCISE 12 (NOVICE, INTERMEDIATE, ADVANCED)

- With the ride in walk, ask the riders to make a transition to halt as their body is lined up with the centre line (rather than the horse's nose or tail). Encourage preparation, for accuracy.

- Halt for 5 seconds, and then walk on again, continuing the half circle and joining the track as they reach the opposite side of the school.

- Explain that the halt should be 'square'. Ask the riders to 'feel' if the halt is square, and then check by using mirrors or looking.

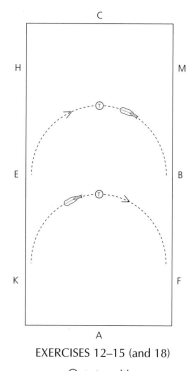

EXERCISES 12–15 (and 18)

Ⓣ = transition

EXERCISE 13 (NOVICE, INTERMEDIATE, ADVANCED)

- With the ride in trot, ask the riders to make a transition to walk as they go over the centre line. Ask for six hind leg steps of walk before making a transition into trot again. (They should be able to feel their hips 'walking' left and right as the horse's hind legs step underneath them.)

- You can ask the riders to be very accurate by asking for three hind leg steps of walk either side of the centre line.

- Explain that different horses require different levels of preparation for their upward and downward transitions. Ask them to tell you whether they think that their horse is forward or backward thinking, and encourage them to think about early preparation.

EXERCISE 14 (NOVICE, INTERMEDIATE, ADVANCED)

- With the ride in trot, ask the riders to make a progressive transition through walk, to halt on the centre line and then, progressively through walk, return to trot.

- Ask the riders to compare the squareness of the halt now, in comparison to the halt in the first exercise. The halt should be squarer now as a result of the horses' improved balance and engagement from the other transitions.

PROBLEMS, Exercises 12–14
- The horse anticipates the exercise and most commonly makes a downward transition as it is

ridden onto the half circle, before the rider asks for it. Make the riders aware of this problem, so that they can ride more strongly, and regain control. Ask the riders to alternate the exercise when they feel that the horse is anticipating, and to maintain the trot around the half circle occasionally. This way the horse will wait for the rider's instructions.

- The shape of the half 20m circle becomes lost and begins to look like a straight line across the school. As a result, the sharp turn off the track unbalances the horse for the transition. Be insistent on the shape of the half 20m circle and explain why.

EXERCISE 15 (INTERMEDIATE, ADVANCED)

- Develop the exercise to include direct transitions. The intermediate rider should be more aware of balance, rhythm, straightness, suppleness and impulsion, and strive to maintain these through 'feel' of the transitions. Thus the horse should have a 'better way of going' than with the novice rider. On corners and the half circles, riders should feel that they are riding from inside leg into outside hand.

- With the ride in trot, ask the riders to make progressive transitions through walk, to halt (on the centre line).

- From halt ask them to make a direct transition to trot. (Remember to explain to the riders how they should prepare for this transition, otherwise the horse is likely to receive a smack from the whip when it does not respond immediately. This is unfair if the transition has been inadequately prepared.)

- Ask the ride to reduce the number of steps in the walk before halt, so that they gradually work towards being able to ride trot to halt directly.

PROBLEMS

- When riding upward and downward transitions directly between halt and trot, the horse may become a fidget in the halt, in anticipation. The riders must realise that although they want the horse to be responsive, it is also their responsibility to keep the horse relaxed. Suggest that they step back in their work and return to progressive exercises, establishing the horse's trust once again, with a pat on the neck in halt.

EXERCISE 16 (INTERMEDIATE, ADVANCED)

- The exercise can now include **canter**.

- Depending on the ability of the riders, the attitude of the horses, and the weather conditions, which may affect the horses, you can ask 1, 2, 4, or all of the ride to ride this exercise at the same time. Ask those waiting to halt in an appropriate place and watch the other riders' transitions.

- Before the riders begin the exercise, explain the preparation required for both upward and downward transitions and when and where it should take place in order to make successful transitions.

- With the ride in trot, ask the riders to canter the

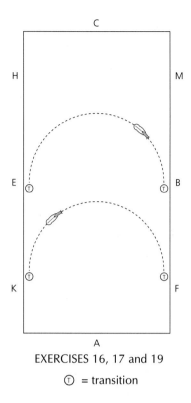

EXERCISES 16, 17 and 19

ⓣ = transition

half 20m circle, making a canter transition as they leave the track, and a transition to trot as they reach the track on the opposite side of the school.

PROBLEMS

- Lack of preparation for the upward and downward canter transitions results in late, unbalanced transitions.

EXERCISES 16–19 (ADVANCED)

- Advanced riders should have a little knowledge of which transitions are going to improve their horse's way of going.

- You can either structure the lesson so that you are in charge of which transitions they ride, as with the intermediates or, after a discussion with each rider individually, you can help them to improve their own horse by tailor-making the exercises for each horse.

EXERCISE 17

- Shortening and lengthening in the trot. (It is a short period of time to do this in the canter.)

EXERCISE 18

- Half transitions in the trot over the centre line. During a half transition in trot, the rider shortens the trot, almost to make a transition to walk, then rides the trot forwards again. This helps to develop engagement of the quarters. (See diagram page 22)

EXERCISE 19

- Ride walk to canter directly, making a progressive transition through trot to walk, lessening the number of trot steps and working towards riding canter to walk directly.

PROBLEMS, Exercises 16–19

- Advanced riders understand accuracy and sometimes sacrifice the horse's correct way of going to achieve it. The horse's way of going must be the priority.

NOTES ON THESE EXERCISES

During these transitions, especially the more demanding ones, the rider must be encouraged to ride the horse forwards. If you observe the horses becoming tense, relay this observation to the riders, and then remedy it for the horses by riding some lengthening work.

If you have a group of riders with varying levels of fitness, these can be demanding exercises to ride. To accommodate this, use only half of the school for the half 20m circle exercises, leaving the other end free for riding a 20m circle. In this way, those that need a 'breather' can walk on an inner track (15m circle) within the 20m circle.

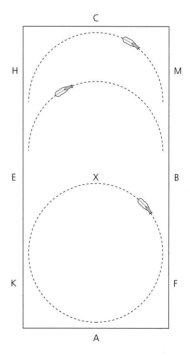

EXERCISES 12–19 alternative arrangement

2. TRANSITIONS ON A FIGURE-OF-EIGHT

RIDER LEVEL Good novice, intermediate and advanced.

AIMS AND BENEFITS

- The figure-of-eight helps to aid suppleness of the horse.
- The frequent changes of rein will make stiff and soft sides more obvious to the rider.
- The rider's awareness of straightness during the transitions will be improved.

EXERCISES

- The figure-of-eight is produced by joining two 20m circles at X.

- Using three poles, place one central pole on the E-B line, over X. The other two go either side of the central pole, creating sufficient space for a horse to pass through. The poles have created transition 'boxes' for either circle on the figure-of-eight.

- Make the ride aware that:

  – The aim is to be able to ride a continuous figure-of-eight, making balanced transitions each time they reach X.

  – One circle, e.g. the A circle, will have priority at X for the change of rein.

  – There must be a period of straightness on the E/B line as they ride the transition and change the bend of the horse.

  – If the transition is poor and the rider wishes to repeat it, he may continue on the same circle until he feels that the transition has improved sufficiently to be able to make a balanced change of rein through X.

EXERCISE 20 (NOVICE, INTERMEDIATE, ADVANCED)

- Start the exercise by asking the riders to ride a continuous figure-of-eight in walk, without any transitions in the 'boxes'. This way you can focus on their ability to change the bend of the horse over X, maintaining balance and rhythm.

- Start to include halt transitions in the boxes.

EXERCISE 21 (NOVICE, INTERMEDIATE, ADVANCED)

- Ask the ride to trot the exercise, riding transitions to walk as they reach the 'boxes'. This development in the exercise will take more time, as there is much to think about and prepare for in a short space of time:
  - preparation for the transition,
  - approach into the 'box',
  - straightness during the transition,
  - riding a good quality walk,
  - change of bend,
  - preparation for the upward transition,
  - riding the transition,
  - establishing rhythm and balance in the trot,
  - shape of the 20m circle.

EXERCISE 22 (NOVICE, INTERMEDIATE, ADVANCED)

- This can be further developed at this level to include a progressive transition to halt in the box, returning to trot, again progressively.

PROBLEMS, Exercises 20–22

- Areas of weakness within this exercise stem from the fact that there is much to prepare for in a short space of time. For this reason it is important that the transitions are simple.

EXERCISES 23 AND 24 (INTERMEDIATE, ADVANCED)

The intermediate rider should be more organised than the novice. As a result, transitions should be

better prepared for and executed in a manner that improves the horse's way of going. The change of bend should be balanced, riding the horse positively from inside leg to outside hand.

EXERCISE 23

- Gradually start to introduce direct transitions through the boxes: halt to trot and trot to halt.

EXERCISE 24

- One or two riders at a time; this exercise can be ridden in canter with a change of lead through trot over X. Halt the rest of the ride in the centre of both circles.

PROBLEMS, Exercises 23 and 24

- Direct downward transitions tend to be ridden with insufficient leg, initially.
- When canter is introduced, the shape of the circle may be lost, but the shape is essential if the rider is to achieve a balanced change of lead through trot.

EXERCISES 25 AND 26 (ADVANCED)

The advanced rider should be riding transitions that aim to maintain the horse's balance and rhythm at all times, using each transition to improve the horse's way of going.

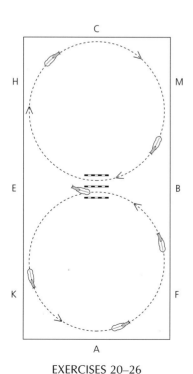

EXERCISES 20–26

EXERCISE 25

- Start to include half transitions in trot over X. (For explanation of half transition, see Exercise 18.)

EXERCISE 26

- By slowly reducing the number of trot steps between canter and walk, the canter exercise can gradually be developed until simple changes (canter to walk to canter) are ridden over X.

PROBLEMS, Exercises 25 and 26
- Riders may need a reminder to use sufficient leg during the transitions.

3. TRANSITIONS AT E, B AND X

RIDER LEVEL Novice, intermediate and advanced.

AIMS AND BENEFITS
- To improve the horse's way of going.
- Feeling the difference between riding a transition on a straight line and a circle, and being taught to ride accordingly.
- Preparation for accuracy.

EXERCISE 27 (NOVICE, INTERMEDIATE, ADVANCED)

- Ask the ride to walk large, riding 20m circles at A and C as they choose.

- Each time they reach E, B or X, riders are to make a transition to halt, remaining in halt for a certain period of time before making a transition to walk again.

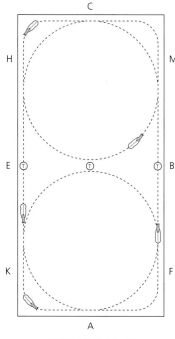

EXERCISES 27–30

ⓣ = transition

EXERCISE 28 (NOVICE, INTERMEDIATE, ADVANCED)

- Repeat the exercise in trot, making a downward transition to walk for a set number of steps before returning to trot again.

PROBLEMS, EXERCISES 27 and 28

- Riders may feel that there is a difference between the transitions ridden on the straight and on the circle. Teach riders to balance the transitions ridden on the circle, where the horses are not supported by the boards.
- For advanced riders the exercise could be made more challenging if ridden on an inner track, where the horse will lose the support of the boards.

EXERCISE 29 (INTERMEDIATE, ADVANCED)

- Make direct transitions between halt and trot at E, B and X.

PROBLEMS

- Any direct transition ridden can lead to tension of both horse and rider. Start by riding the transitions progressively and gradually reduce the number of walk steps

EXERCISE 30 (including canter, for good INTERMEDIATE and ADVANCED riders)

- Explain the reason for asking for canter in a corner or on a circle – that it helps to influence the horse's lead leg.
- Explain how to ask for the correct lead leg for the direction of travel while on a straight line, i.e. when on the right rein you would like the rider to ask for the right lead canter. The explanation should include:

  - adequate preparation,

  - correct application of the aids,

  - having slight inside flexion, with the horse working slightly more into the outside rein, as they would on a circle or on a corner.

- With one or two riders working at a time, ask them to ride canter transitions at X, E and B, making downward transitions to trot wherever appropriate in between.

PROBLEMS

- For any rider who struggles repeatedly to achieve the correct lead leg on the straight line, ask them to leg yield from the three-quarter line to the track and, at the moment they reach the track, to ask for canter. This should encourage the rider to move the horse into the outside hand, helping to reinforce the rider's aids. You can then gradually reduce the number of leg yield steps, until they have the feel and co-ordination to ride the exercise correctly.

4 CIRCLES

The circle is usually the first school figure that riders learn. It is the most basic shape taught, and a figure that riders will use throughout their riding career. Circles are highly versatile in that a variety of concepts can be taught and learned using them, from riding the shape accurately, to developing the feel of working the horse from the inside leg into the outside hand.

BEGINNER

- The aim when teaching the beginner is to encourage a good shape and size of 20m circle at A, C and E/B in walk and trot.

- Develop co-ordination of the aids.

NOVICE

- The novice needs to develop a feel for the shape and size of 15m and 20m circles and where they can be ridden in the school.

- The rider should be taught about straightness and relative straightness. (Straightness refers to the horse being straight on a straight line, with the hind legs remaining directly behind the front legs. Relative straightness refers to the horse's straightness on a curve, for example, a circle. From nose to tail, the horse's body should follow the line of the circle.)

- The novice rider can start to ride the circle using the correct aids to encourage the horse to bend around the circle. These aids are:

Inside leg creates bend and forward movement.

Outside leg is used slightly behind the girth to encourage the hindquarters of the horse to bend around the inside leg. The outside leg also supports the inside leg by helping to generate forward movement.

Inside rein encourages inside flexion through the horse's neck. (In the beginning, the inside rein can be opened slightly to achieve this.)

Outside rein controls the speed and the amount of bend.

INTERMEDIATE

- Intermediate riders should start to include 10m circles in their work, the emphasis being on maintaining the balance and rhythm of the walk or trot.

- They should develop a greater understanding of bend and begin to develop a feel for the horse's correct way of going, working from inside leg to outside hand.

ADVANCED

- Advanced riders further need to develop their

ability to maintain the horse's correct way of going through walk, trot and canter on 10m, 15m and 20m circles, depending on the horse's level of training.

AIMS AND BENEFITS

RIDER

- Accuracy.
- Spatial awareness.
- Co-ordination of the aids.
- Feel between leg and hand.

HORSE

- Suppleness.
- Straightness.
- Rhythm.
- Balance.
- Engagement.

WALK AND TROT EXERCISES IN RIDE AND SEMI-OPEN ORDER

1. 20M CIRCLES FOR BEGINNERS

RIDER LEVEL Beginner and novice.

AIMS AND BENEFITS

- Progression from riding large.
- Steering.
- Confidence.
- Spatial awareness.

EXERCISE 31

- Mark out a 20m circle at A or C using cones.
- Teach the ride the location of X.
- With the ride in walk on the 20m circle, lead file in succession trot to the rear of the ride on the circle.
- Repeat on the other rein.

EXERCISE 32

- As above, trot in twos, threes, fours, and then the whole ride together.

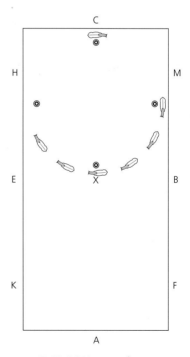

EXERCISES 31 and 32

- Some horses that do not find being lead file easy may cut across the circle to the rear of the ride. The instructor may need to support or use leaders for child riders.
- As riders learn co-ordination, the aids become more refined, but early on the rider may over- or under-turn around the circle.
- With a good horse and rider as lead file, teaching circles is often easier as a ride, so that both horses and riders alike have someone to follow.

EXERCISE 33

- As both the above exercises, but with the 20m circle marked out at E/B. (This is a harder exercise as there is little support from the boards.)

PROBLEMS

- Before this exercise is ridden, ensure the riders are competent at riding 20m circles at A and C.
- The riders will need to be confident at steering to achieve a 20m circle at E/B successfully.

EXERCISE 34

- Whole ride going large in walk.

- Lead file in succession trot to the rear of the ride, trotting a 20m circle at either A or C, whichever is the free end of the school. (At first, with children, you may need to tell them where to circle to prevent them from choosing the wrong end!)

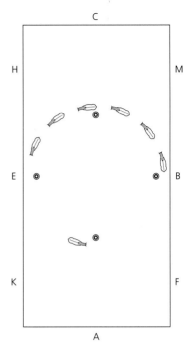

EXERCISE 33

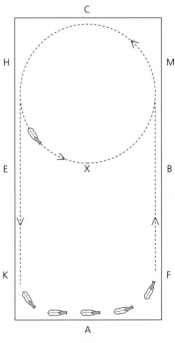

EXERCISE 34

PROBLEMS

- Horses and ponies differ in their level of independence and, as a result, some are more difficult to steer than others when they are not following the ride. You may need to assist in the beginning.

2. DIVIDING THE RIDE ONTO TWO 20M CIRCLES (NOVICE)

RIDER LEVEL Novice.

AIMS AND BENEFITS

- Developing a feel for riding a circle.
- Suppleness.

EXERCISE 35

- Divide the ride so that they are on two 20m circles at A and C on opposing reins, in walk. (It is safer to have the horses approaching X from the same direction rather than head on.)

- Number the riders 1 to 4 on each circle. In numerical order, taking one circle at a time, ask them to trot to the rear of the ride on their circle.

EXERCISE 36

- As above, with both circles working at the same time, e.g. number 1 riders on both circles trot to the rear of the ride.

EXERCISE 37

- As above, asking the next lead file to trot when the one in front is half a circle ahead. (This helps to keep all riders focused.)

EXERCISE 38

- Trot both rides together on their circles.

PROBLEMS, Exercises 35–38

- Horses may fall in or out on the circles – encourage the riders to maintain the contact and use the leg.

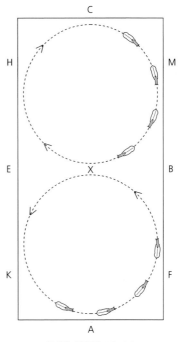

EXERCISES 35–38

EXERCISE 39

- Halting each numerical pair at X in turn, ask them to create a 'password'. This can be whispered to each other each time they meet at X. (If there is an odd number, the instructor will need to stand in at X as the other half of a pair!)

- Firstly in walk, ask the riders to pass at X in their pairs, whispering their passwords as they meet at X. Explain that they have to watch their partner on the other circle and try to be a mirror image of where their partner is, while maintaining their distance in the ride.

EXERCISE 40

- If this is achieved in walk, try it in trot.

PROBLEMS, Exercises 39 and 40

- Although seemingly simple, this exercise challenges children's spatial awareness. The instructor will need to coax riders into position so that they meet in their pairs over X.

EXERCISE 41

- To make this exercise more difficult, spread each ride out so that they have a quarter of a circle between them. They must maintain their distances and meet their partner at X.

- (Children enjoy using passwords and it offers added incentive to meet at X. For adults this is unnecessary, unless you have a particularly fun group!)

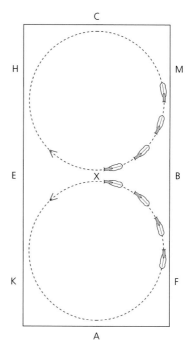

EXERCISES 39 and 40

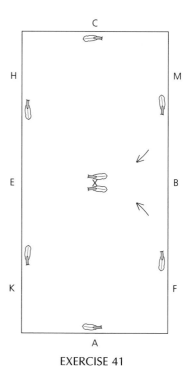

EXERCISE 41

PROBLEMS

- Ensure riders are secure in the previous exercise before riding this one, which adds the extra dimension of maintaining a distance within the ride.

3. DIVIDING THE RIDE ONTO TWO 20M CIRCLES (NOVICE AND INTERMEDIATE)

RIDER LEVEL Good novice and intermediate.

AIM AND BENEFITS

- Rhythm.
- Balance.
- Bend.
- Correct application of the aids for a circle.

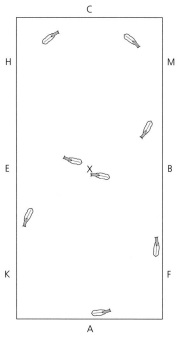

EXERCISE 42

EXERCISE 42

- Explain the correct aids for riding a circle. (See guide for teaching novices, page 30.)

- In walk, offer help to each individual. This should include the positioning of the legs and hands, and the correct feel of both.

- Once achieved in the walk, progress to trotting the riders in a semi-open order on the circle. Riders should aim for consistency of feel between leg and hand, and the curve of the horse on the circle.

- Offer regular changes of rein and ask the riders to tell you which side they think is the horse's stiff side and which is his soft side.

PROBLEMS

- Initially, co-ordination of the aids is difficult. Riders have a tendency to ride off the inside rein and forget about their outside aids.

EXERCISE 43

- With the ride in semi-open order, explain how to decrease the size of the circle to 15m, and then to 10m, within the 20m circle.

- In walk first, and then trot, ask the ride to spiral in and out between the three sizes of circle.

- This can progress to leg yielding from 10m to 15m to 20m.

PROBLEMS

- Maintaining the shape of the 15m and 10m circles is a potential problem for any rider not applying the aids correctly. The horses may have a tendency to fall in or out.

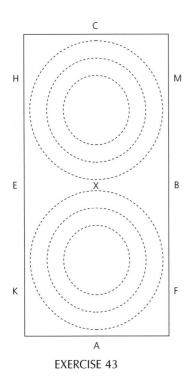

EXERCISE 43

EXERCISE 44

- With the ride in trot on both circles in semi-open order, ask the riders to count the number of strides on both halves of the circle. The number should be the same.

- Decrease the size of the circle to 15m and 10m and repeat. If rhythm, balance, length of stride and shape of circle have been maintained there should be a relationship between the number of strides on each circle, e.g. 7, 6, 5 strides on each half of 20m, 15m and 10m circles.

PROBLEMS

- Any loss of rhythm, balance, length of stride and shape of circle will affect the horse's correct way of going. Ask the riders to try to assess what they have lost and how to rectify it.

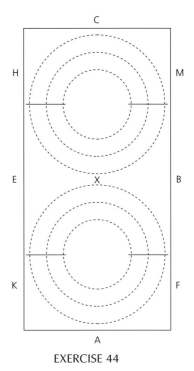

EXERCISE 44

WALK AND TROT EXERCISES IN OPEN ORDER

1. 20M, 15M AND 10M CIRCLES

RIDER LEVEL Intermediate and advanced.

AIMS AND BENEFITS
- Improving the rider's ability.
- Improving the horse's way of going.
- Suppleness.

EXERCISE 45

- Ride to go large and ride 20m circles at A and C.

- Ask them to try to establish quality in their work by using transitions in halt, walk and trot to improve the horse's responses and engagement.

PROBLEMS
- Insist on the quality of the circles and transitions.

EXERCISE 46

- As above, riding 15m circles at A and C.

- This should increase the horse's engagement further, so long as the rider has the ability to maintain the shape and size of the circle, the balance and rhythm and the impulsion and bend.

PROBLEMS
- Loss of shape of the circle often results in a loss of straightness in the horse.

EXERCISE 45

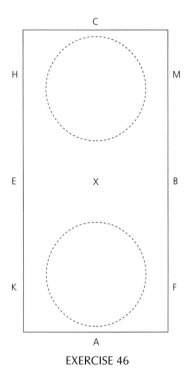

EXERCISE 46

EXERCISE 47

- As above, riding 10m circles at A, E, C and B.

- This is a far more demanding exercise for both horse and rider, and frequent rest periods are required.

PROBLEMS

- Using excess inside rein, when instead the horse should be moving into the outside rein from the inside leg.
- Horse loses impulsion due to the rider not using sufficient leg.
- Loss of balance and rhythm.

2. SIX 10M CIRCLES

RIDER LEVEL Good intermediate and advanced.

AIMS AND BENEFITS
- Suppleness.
- Balance.
- Rhythm.
- Engagement.
- Co-ordination of the aids.
- Accuracy.

EXERCISE 48

- Place cones at D, X and G, to stop the circles from overlapping. Ensure that the riders know they should come on the inside of the cones. All the circles ridden will be of 10m diameter.

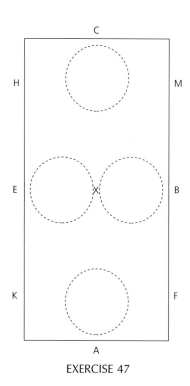

EXERCISE 47

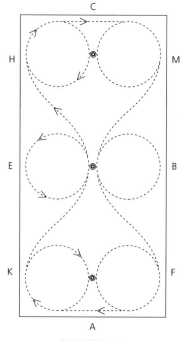

EXERCISE 48

- Start this exercise in walk. (It may be necessary for you to walk it on foot to enable the riders to visualise what you are explaining.)

- If starting on the right rein, for example, ride a right circle at K. On completion of the circle, walk to X, as if on a 10m shallow loop. At X ride a left circle. On completion of that circle, continue the loop to H. At H ride a right circle. Going large from H, repeat on the other side of the school, starting at M.

- Once the riders are confident in the walk, progress to the trot.

- It is a demanding exercise for both horse and rider. Offer frequent rests, at which point each rider can discuss how they feel that the exercise is improving the horse and any areas of weakness within the work.

- Riders on the circles have right of way.

PROBLEMS

- Lack of preparation from the rider, resulting in loss of balance and rhythm in the work. If ridden by inexperienced riders, this exercise can result in a deterioration of the horse's way of going.
- To make the exercise easier, walk certain circles and trot the others. This gives riders the opportunity to reorganise themselves and slows the exercise down.

CANTER EXERCISES IN RIDE ORDER

1. CANTER WORK WITH THE RIDE DIVIDED ONTO TWO 20M CIRCLES

RIDER LEVEL Novice and intermediate.

AIMS AND BENEFITS

- Maintaining the shape and size of a 20m circle in canter.
- Rhythm.
- Balance.
- Confidence.

EXERCISE 49

- One circle at a time, ask the ride to trot on their 20m circle.

- Lead file in succession makes a transition to canter at a specific point, and maintains the canter to the rear of the ride on the circle. (With novice riders it is best to ask for canter between X and the boards, as the horse will begin the canter supported by the boards. This gives novice riders time to organise themselves in the canter.)

- Depending on the ability of the ride, this may require help from the instructor.

- With intermediate groups, insist on accuracy of the transitions, using adequate preparation, with an accurate circle, maintaining balance and rhythm throughout.

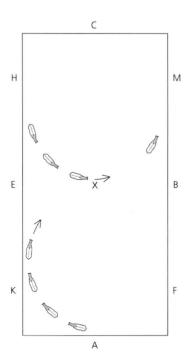

EXERCISES 49 and 50

EXERCISE 51

- Assuming that there are four on each circle, ask two riders to halt in the middle of the circle, or walk on a 10m circle, while the other two trot on their circle with half a circle distance between them.

- Either working one or both circles at a time, give the riders who are trotting the command to canter.

- The riders can be given a period of time to canter before returning to trot, e.g. one circle, returning to trot at the point at which the canter transition was made.

- Repeat once or twice more, enabling riders to make improvements, before swapping over and moving onto the riders who have been halted.

PROBLEMS

- Lack of preparation for both upward and downward transitions.
- Horse falling in or out on the circle.

EXERCISE 50

- For intermediate groups, this exercise can be ridden working both circles at the same time, depending on weather conditions and horses' temperaments.

PROBLEMS

- Safety has priority. Before starting to work more than one rider in canter at the same time, you must be confident that all will maintain control.

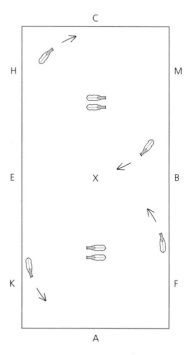

EXERCISES 51 and 52

PROBLEMS

- Horses cantering tend to fall in to the middle of the circle towards the others in halt.

EXERCISE 52

- The above exercise can be ridden with emphasis on balance, rhythm, impulsion and shape of the circle, by asking the riders to count the number of strides on each half of the circle. The number should be the same.

PROBLEMS

- The number of strides is not the same. The reason for this must be assessed and corrected.

CANTER EXERCISES IN OPEN ORDER

1. CANTER EXERCISES WITH THE RIDE DIVIDED ONTO TWO 15M CIRCLES

RIDER LEVEL Intermediate and advanced.

AIMS AND BENEFITS

- Independence.
- Rhythm.
- Balance.
- Accuracy.

EXERCISE 53

- Divide the ride onto two 20m circles at A and C, both on the same rein.

- Decrease the size of the circles to 15m.

- With the ride in walk, ask one rider at a time from each circle to leg yield out onto a 20m circle, at which point they make a transition to trot.

- When they feel that they are prepared, the riders then make a transition to canter.

- They canter one complete circle around the other riders, making a transition to trot at the point where they started cantering.

- Making a balanced transition to walk, they can return to their position on the 15m circle.

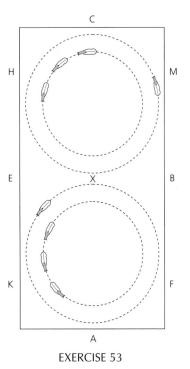

EXERCISE 53

• Continue the exercise with the rest of the ride.

PROBLEMS

• The horse falls in on the circle towards the rest of the ride and loses the canter. The rider must take control of the situation and encourage the horse to listen by riding strongly with the aids.

EXERCISE 54

• As above, but this time as each rider makes the transition to canter, they go large.

• Circle 20m around the riders at the opposite end of the school.

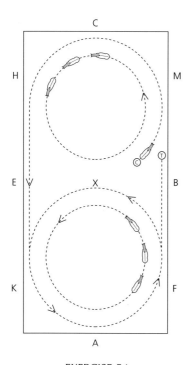

EXERCISE 54

Ⓣ = trot transition   Ⓒ = canter transition

• Riders continue large and return to their own circle.

• They can make a progressive transition through trot to walk and return to their place.

PROBLEMS

• While going large, the canter becomes long and flat and the horse may break into trot if not kept between leg and hand.

• Loss of balance and rhythm in the canter.

2. WALK TO CANTER FROM A 5M CIRCLE

RIDER LEVEL Advanced.

AIMS AND BENEFITS

• Accuracy.

• Preparation.

• Co-ordination of the aids.

EXERCISE 55

• With the ride divided onto two 20m circles, have two riders halted in the centre of each circle, with two walking on each circle, spread out evenly.

• The riders in walk ride a 5m circle towards the halted riders.

• At the moment they rejoin the 20m circle, they make a direct transition from walk to canter.

• They canter one complete circle, returning progressively to walk.

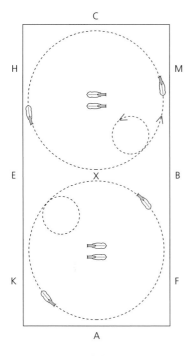

EXERCISE 55

EXERCISE 56

- A development of the previous exercise.

- The riders canter large, riding a 2–3m shallow loop along the long side.

- On reaching the circle at the opposite end of the school, they circle 20m before returning progressively or directly to walk.

PROBLEMS
- The exercise is difficult. Build the layers into the exercise gradually, which may take time.
- During the shallow loop in canter, insist that the bend remains over the lead leg.

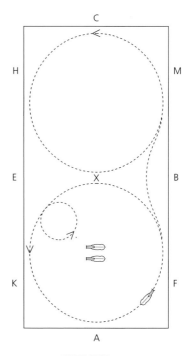

EXERCISE 56

- The canter to walk transition can gradually be made more direct by spiralling the canter circle down to 12–15m, helping to collect the canter before asking for walk.

PROBLEMS
- The 5m circle helps to prepare the horses for the transition to canter. Ensure that it is executed correctly and with energy, as often it is not ridden with sufficient leg.
- Inadequate preparation for the transitions.

5 SCHOOL FIGURES

School figures help to develop an understanding of 'feel' that otherwise may not be achieved. They also add variety to the work for riders, horses and instructors and help to develop a well-educated rider. As riders develop they learn that school figures are used to improve the horse's way of going.

BEGINNER

Beginners are introduced to the 20m circle as their first school figure. See Chapter 4, Circles.

NOVICE

In addition to circles, novice riders are introduced to further school figures, which are initially used as tools to improve the co-ordination of the aids so that the shape can be ridden accurately in the walk and trot. As the riding ability improves, figures should be ridden with consideration of balance, rhythm, impulsion, suppleness, straightness, constantly with regard for the rider's position.

INTERMEDIATE

The intermediate rider further develops the skills learned at novice level. The rider should feel when the horse is going in a correct way and start to understand why and how this is lost, and how to correct it.

ADVANCED

The advanced rider should further develop the ability to analyse the horse's way of going, and use the school figures to make improvements. By using the figures in a more complex way, or in a higher pace, their understanding and feel will improve as the exercise becomes more demanding.

AIMS AND BENEFITS

RIDER
- Co-ordination of the aids.
- Feel.
- Accuracy.
- Position.

HORSE
- Rhythm.
- Balance.
- Suppleness.
- Straightness.
- Bend.
- Impulsion.
- Engagement.

CIRCLES

See Chapter 4.

FIGURES-OF-EIGHT

Figures-of-eight encourage riders to ride between leg and hand to achieve the change of bend through X. They can be ridden in two ways:

• two 20m circles joined together at X,

• riding across the diagonals KXM and FXH.

The following exercises assume the method of the two 20m circles joined at X.

1. AS A RIDE ON A FIGURE-OF-EIGHT

RIDER LEVEL Novice.

AIMS AND BENEFITS
• Accuracy of shape.
• Rhythm.
• Balance.

EXERCISE 57

• In walk, ride a figure-of-eight.

• Explain how to change the horse's bend over X.

EXERCISE 58

• Lead file trot in succession to the rear of the ride.

• If the lead file and the ride meet at X, the lead file has priority and the ride will halt to let them continue. The instructor may need to take control and not leave the decision to the ride.

EXERCISE 59

• Trot as a ride on the figure-of-eight.

PROBLEMS, Exercises 57–59
• The shape is inaccurate towards the rear of the ride. Encourage riders to work independently or, for children, ask them to ride towards the outside hind leg of the horse in front.

• Inaccurately ridden change of bend over X, leading to the horse falling in or out.

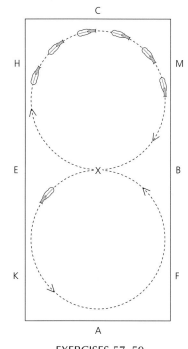

EXERCISES 57–59

2. FIGURE-OF-EIGHT IN OPEN ORDER

RIDER LEVEL Novice, intermediate and advanced.

AIMS AND BENEFITS
- Riding a balanced change of rein over X.

EXERCISE 60

- Working in open order in walk, ask the ride to focus on the bend on the circle.

- Once any rider feels that they can achieve the bend consistently, they can change circles, focusing on accurately changing bend as they ride through X.

- The aim is to be able to ride a continuous figure-of-eight maintaining the correct bend at all times.

EXERCISE 61

- As above, in trot, including the aim to improve the horse's balance and rhythm.

EXERCISE 62

- As the above two exercises, starting to include a transition to walk over X as the riders change circle, returning to trot once they have changed the bend.

- Develop the exercise into a transition to halt at X, and then either a progressive or a direct transition to trot.

PROBLEMS, Exercises 60–62
- Riders try to work through the exercises too quickly, and as a result find the latter exercises difficult.
- Riders lose focus of the original aim, bend, and as a result, lose their balance and rhythm.
- Loss of balance and rhythm during the transition – keep the leg on.

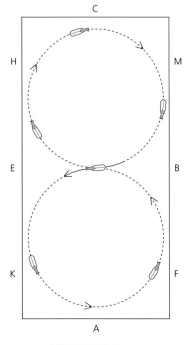

EXERCISES 60–62

EXERCISE 63 (CANTER)

- One or two at a time, ask the riders to canter their figure-of-eight making a change of lead leg through trot over X. (The rest of the ride can halt in the middle of their circles.)

- For intermediate groups, this can develop into a direct transition from walk to canter, and then a progressive return to walk through trot.

- Advanced groups can work towards simple changes over X directly between walk and canter.

PROBLEMS

- The progress made in the trot does not always carry over into the canter. Emphasise that the same is required of the canter as the trot.

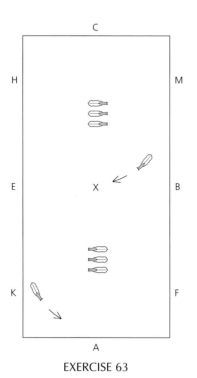

EXERCISE 63

SHALLOW LOOPS

Shallow loops are a superb suppling exercise and it is simple to vary the level of difficulty for each level of rider.

1. 5M SHALLOW LOOPS AS A RIDE

RIDER LEVEL Novice.

AIMS AND BENEFITS
- Control.
- Accuracy.

EXERCISES 64–66

- Use cones to highlight the deepest part of the loop opposite E and B and, if necessary, opposite K, F, M and H to aid the riding of corners.

EXERCISE 64

- Walk the shallow loops as a ride together. Be insistent that the riders use the letters accurately and do not cut corners.

EXERCISE 65

- Lead file in succession trot large, riding a 5m shallow loop on both long sides of the school.

EXERCISE 66

- Whole ride trot 5m loops on both long sides of the school.

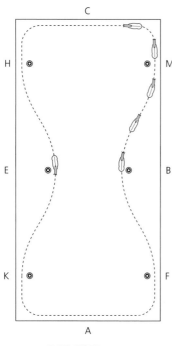

EXERCISES 64–66

EXERCISE 67

- Organise the ride into open order.

- Use cones to assist the riders to achieve the correct shape.

- Walk the loops, concentrating on the correct shape.

- Trot the loops, concentrating on the correct shape.

EXERCISE 68

- For more experienced novices, explain the change of bend within the loops.

- Begin the exercise in walk and progress to trot.

PROBLEMS, Exercises 64–66
- As with any school figure ridden as a ride, those at the rear of the ride tend to lose the shape. Encourage accuracy.

2. 5M SHALLOW LOOPS IN OPEN ORDER (NOVICE)

RIDER LEVEL Novice.

AIMS AND BENEFITS
- This is a lovely exercise to use for riders new to open order, as it can be as simple or as complicated as the instructor makes it.

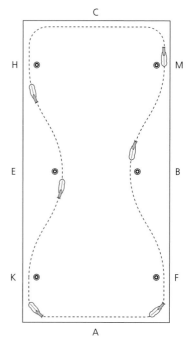

EXERCISES 67, 68 and 70

PROBLEMS, Exercises 67 and 68

- Loss of shape.
- Frequent changes of bend may initially be hard to achieve.
- Inaccuracy in corners.

3. SHALLOW LOOPS IN OPEN ORDER (INTERMEDIATE AND ADVANCED)

RIDER LEVEL Intermediate, advanced.

AIMS AND BENEFITS

- To improve suppleness.
- Co-ordination of the aids.

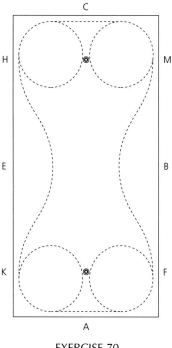

EXERCISE 70

EXERCISE 69

- As exercise 68, with focus on the rider's preparation and subsequent changes of bend on the loop.

- Focus also on the maintenance of rhythm and balance throughout.

PROBLEMS

- Lack of preparation for the change of bend.

EXERCISE 70

- Ride a 10m circle at the beginning and end of each shallow loop in walk and trot.

- Place cones at D and G to prevent the 10m circles from overlapping.

PROBLEMS, Exercise 70

- Horse loses impulsion on the 10m circle.

EXERCISE 71

- Ride a 5m loop with 10m circles on one side of the school, and two 3m loops on the other side of the school. This exercise really makes good riders think and become very accurate, and therefore it improves the horse.

PROBLEMS

- Lack of preparation for the two 3m loops, which do seem to come upon the rider very quickly.

EXERCISE 72 (CANTER)

- For the advanced rider, cantering a shallow loop is a good introduction to counter canter.

- One or two at a time, with the rest of the ride halted on the centre line, the riders can canter their shallow loops. They do not have to ride a loop on each side of the school, but only when they have the quality of the canter to do so.

- The horse's bend must stay over the lead leg at all times.

PROBLEMS

- The rider steers the horse back into the track with the reins, losing the correct bend. Riders must maintain the correct bend and use the legs to help to guide the horse around the loop.

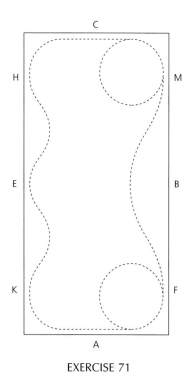

EXERCISE 71

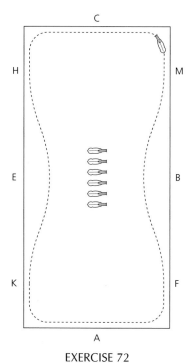

EXERCISE 72

SERPENTINES

Exercises using serpentines are a wonderful aid in teaching balance and rhythm. It is obvious to the rider when balance and rhythm are lost, and a dramatic improvement is evident when serpentines are ridden correctly.

1. THREE- OR FOUR-LOOP SERPENTINES IN RIDE ORDER

RIDER LEVEL Novice, intermediate and advanced.

AIMS AND BENEFITS

- Rhythm.
- Balance.
- Straightness.
- Bend.

EXERCISE 73

- For novice riders it is advisable to use poles or cones to mark out the serpentine – mentally dividing the school into three or four sections is not easy for inexperienced riders.

- Explain the areas where the horse should be straight, and where the line curves.

- Ride initially in walk, then in trot.

- Ask the ride to decide where the horse's rhythm changes, then work to improve.

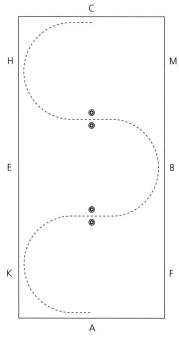

EXERCISES 73–75 (as three loops)

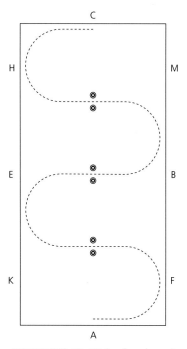

EXERCISES 73–75 (as four loops)

EXERCISE 74

- For intermediate and advanced groups, use the serpentine as a tool at the beginning of the lesson to assess rhythm and balance.

- Assess where rhythm and balance are lost, and why, and work to improve.

- Once improved, move onto a different exercise to continue the work on balance and rhythm in open order.

PROBLEMS, Exercises 73 and 74
- Explain rhythm in simple terms, especially to children. Although the word 'speed' is excluded from equestrian vocabulary, and never substitutes for rhythm, children may initially relate to this more. 'Regularity of the beat' may also be of help when explaining rhythm.
- Loss of bend and straightness will affect the horse's balance and rhythm.

EXERCISE 75

- With advanced riders during a private lesson, **canter** work can be developed on the serpentine.

- Canter work on the serpentine can follow directly on from changes of lead through trot or walk on a figure-of-eight. Change the lead leg through trot or walk on the serpentine.

PROBLEMS
- Lack of preparation leads to late transitions, affecting the whole exercise.

CENTRE LINE

The centre line is ridden at the start and finish of every dressage test. Some riders may aspire to compete one day, and this is a valuable lesson to have taught. For those who enjoy their jumping, it can obviously be linked to the rider's ability to ride a straight line to a fence, from a good turn. It improves riders' preparation and develops an awareness of straightness.

1. CENTRE LINE WORK IN RIDE ORDER – WALK AND TROT

RIDER LEVEL Good tiny tots, novice and intermediate.

AIMS AND BENEFITS
- Good turns.
- Straightness.

EXERCISES 76 AND 77

- Place a pole on either side of the centre line at X.

EXERCISE 76

- In walk, the ride turns up the centre line from A to C every time.

- Rear file in succession halts at X and waits for the rest of the ride to catch up with them before walking on as lead file, and choosing whether the ride turns left or right at C. (If riders are unsure of left and right, use M and H for direction instead.)

The rider will need to glance behind to observe the ride's progress.

EXERCISE 77

• As above, but this time with the ride in trot, rear file in succession makes a transition to walk at X, before continuing in trot as lead file as the rest of the ride catches up.

PROBLEMS, Exercises 75 and 76

• Ponies that are not 'natural leaders' may not be easy lead files. The instructor may have to support.

• Children rarely understand the value of riding good turns. Initially, two cones near A and C on the centre line will help to prevent the cutting of corners.

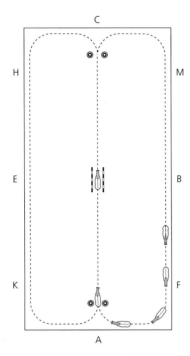

EXERCISES 76 and 77

2. CENTRE LINE WORK IN OPEN ORDER – WALK AND TROT

RIDER LEVEL Intermediate and advanced.

AIMS AND BENEFITS

• Good turns.
• Straightness.

EXERCISES 78 AND 79

• In open order, riders turn up the centre line at A. Give one rein priority at A. Track either right or left at C.

EXERCISE 78

• Starting in walk, riders make a transition to halt at E or B for 5 seconds.

EXERCISE 79

• In trot, there are a variety of exercise that can be ridden along the long sides:

  – walk transition at E or B for a number of strides,

  – shortening or lengthening,

  – shallow loops,

  – leg yield towards X and back out again by the end of the long side,

  – walk transition just before E or B, into a 5m circle at E or B. Continue in trot on returning to E or B.

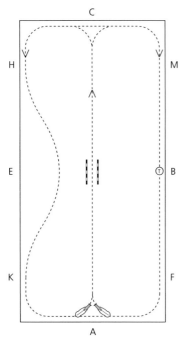

EXERCISES 78 and 79

ⓣ = transition

PROBLEMS, Exercises 78 and 79

- Lack of preparation for the turn onto the centre line, leading to under- or overshooting the turn.
- The rider does not ask for straightness on the centre line. The horse must continually be channelled between leg and hand.
- Approaching C, the horse wavers left and right because the rider has not indicated which way they are going. Encourage the riders to see this from the horse's point of view. The rider is taking the horse towards a wall, and must imperceptibly tell the horse which way they are going to turn, to prevent the horse from making a decision for self-preservation.

3. CANTER ON THE CENTRE LINE

RIDER LEVEL Novice, intermediate and advanced.

AIMS AND BENEFITS
- Asking for canter on a straight line.
- Recognising the leading leg.

EXERCISES 80 AND 81

- For all these exercises it is important that the rider returns to trot before turning up the centre line. Horses can become long and flat in the canter along the long sides, which makes the turn onto the centre line dangerous if ridden in canter.

EXERCISE 80 (NOVICE)

- The ride turns up the centre line at A in trot.
- All but lead file, walk at X.
- Lead file continue in trot and choose to turn left or right at C.
- Canter in the corner following C.
- Maintain the canter to the end of the long side.
- Trot at the end of the long side and turn up the centre line, joining the rear of the ride.
- The ride follows in the direction of the lead file, and trots as the lead file joins the ride, at the rear.

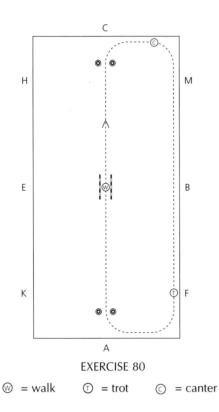

EXERCISE 80

ⓦ = walk   ⓣ = trot   ⓒ = canter

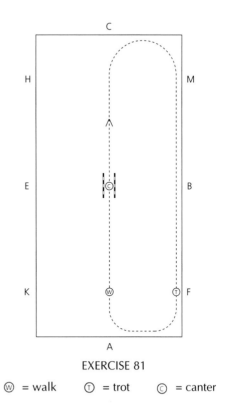

EXERCISE 81

ⓦ = walk   ⓣ = trot   ⓒ = canter

PROBLEMS

- Lack of preparation for the turns, leading to a loss of balance and rhythm.
- Aids unclear.
- Loss of position during either turn.

EXERCISE 81 (INTERMEDIATE AND ADVANCED)

- As above, but the ride returns to walk at D. Lead file makes a transition to canter on a named lead leg at X.

- When asking for the canter, aids must be clear, with slight bend to inside to achieve the desired lead leg. The preceding corner must be balanced and accurate.

- Intermediates may not be as co-ordinated or prepared as advanced riders, and may not achieve the lead leg desired. It is important that the horse turns in the direction of the lead leg, which may need to be called out by the instructor.

- The turn from centre line to the track is difficult, as it is the equivalent of riding a half 10m circle in canter. Riders must sit back and balance the horse between leg and hand to maintain the canter.

PROBLEMS

- Lack of preparation.

- Aids unclear.
- Incorrect bend during the canter transition, possibly resulting in the incorrect lead leg.
- Loss of position during either turn.

RIDING LARGE

Often, little attention is paid to the way that we ride large. The exercises that follow help riders to appreciate how to ride large correctly.

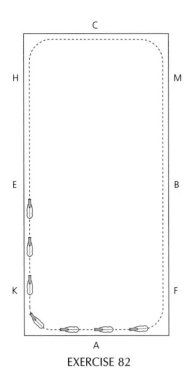

EXERCISE 82

1. RIDING LARGE

RIDER LEVEL Novice, intermediate and advanced.

AIMS AND BENEFITS
- Awareness of rhythm.
- Balance.
- Impulsion.
- Bend.
- Suppleness.
- Straightness.

EXERCISE 82

- Either as a ride or in open order, ask the riders to assess the horse's rhythm and balance in walk and trot while going large.
- Where does the rhythm and balance change?
- Work to make improvements.
- Talk about riding corners.
- Canter the ride large, one at a time.
- Ask if the horse loses the rhythm and balance in the same places as in trot.
- Work to improve.

PROBLEMS
- Rider loses position in the corners, affecting the horse's balance.
- Rider does not prepare for or ride the corners correctly.
- Rider does not actively try to maintain the rhythm.
- Rider has little awareness of rhythm.
- The problems in trot are often exaggerated in the canter, and the corners are less balanced because

the rider allows the horse to become long and flat along the long sides.

2. RIDING LARGE ON AN INNER TRACK

RIDER LEVEL Intermediate and advanced.

AIMS AND BENEFITS
- To encourage riders to ride positively and be in control of every footfall of the horse.

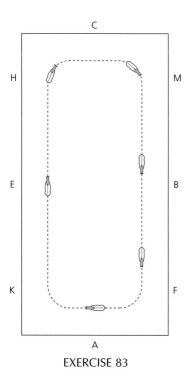

EXERCISE 83

EXERCISE 83

- In open order the ride is to walk and trot going large on an inner track.

- Riders should quickly become aware of two ideas:

  (1) the horses are used to being supported by the boards,

  (2) the horses are drawn to the boards like magnets.

- Work to improve the riders' ability to prepare and ride positively for what they want, with use of the outside aids.

- Repeat the exercise in canter, working with one or two riders at a time.

PROBLEMS
- Lack of co-ordination of the aids.
- Waiting for the horse to go wrong and then working to correct it, rather than riding positively in the first place.

6 CHANGES OF REIN

Ridden in every lesson, changes of rein can be taught as a lesson in their own right. If riders are taught how to use the letters correctly from the start, they will find that changes become natural, as should balanced turns. Changes of rein vary in difficulty. Try to use different changes to add interest and variety, as well as to develop the education of the rider.

BEGINNER
Teach beginners how to use the letters correctly; leaving the track as their body is lined up with the letter, and aiming to arrive at the track slightly before the letter. Use simple changes of rein in the walk, and insist upon accuracy.

NOVICE
Concentrate on the turn (balance, rhythm, impulsion), straightness and accuracy. Riders can begin to ride changes of rein in trot.

INTERMEDIATE
Use more complex changes of rein to further develop co-ordination of the aids and accuracy.

Simple changes of rein in the canter can be introduced.

ADVANCED
When working in open order, encourage riders to make their own changes of rein to complement the work that they are doing. Increase the level of difficulty of the changes of rein in the canter, and begin to introduce a few strides of counter-canter into the work.

AIMS AND BENEFITS

RIDER
- Accuracy.
- Co-ordination of the aids.
- Working towards riding a dressage test.

HORSE
- Rhythm.
- Balance.
- Suppleness.
- Straightness.
- Impulsion.

EXERCISE 84 – LONG DIAGONAL

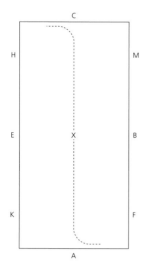

BEGINNER – walk. NOVICE – walk, trot.
INTERMEDIATE – walk, trot, canter.
ADVANCED – walk, trot, canter.

EXERCISE 85 – SHORT DIAGONAL

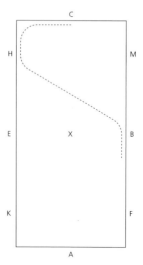

BEGINNER – walk. NOVICE – walk, trot.
INTERMEDIATE – walk, trot, canter.
ADVANCED – walk, trot, canter (continue in
counter-canter to the end of the long side).

EXERCISE 86 – CENTRE LINE

BEGINNER – walk. NOVICE – walk, trot.
INTERMEDIATE – walk, trot.
ADVANCED – walk, trot.

EXERCISE 87 – E–B

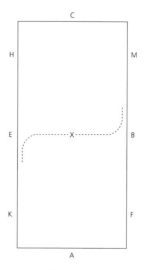

BEGINNER – walk. NOVICE – walk, trot.
INTERMEDIATE – walk, trot.
ADVANCED – walk, trot.

EXERCISE 88 – TWO HALF 20M CIRCLES

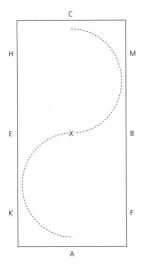

NOVICE – walk, trot. INTERMEDIATE – walk, trot.
ADVANCED – walk, trot, canter.

EXERCISE 89 – HALF 15M CIRCLE INCLINING TO THE TRACK

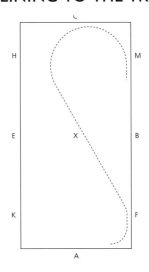

NOVICE – walk, trot. INTERMEDIATE – walk, trot.
ADVANCED – walk, trot, canter.

EXERCISE 90 – HALF 10M CIRCLE INCLINING TO B/E OR M/K/F/H

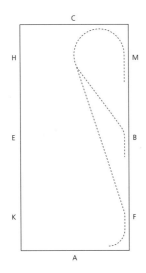

NOVICE – walk, trot. INTERMEDIATE – walk, trot.
ADVANCED – walk, trot, canter (continue in
counter-canter to the end of the long side).

EXERCISE 91 – TWO HALF 10M CIRCLES

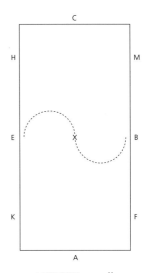

NOVICE – walk.
INTERMEDIATE – walk, trot.
ADVANCED – walk, trot.

EXERCISE 92 – FOUR-LOOP SERPENTINE

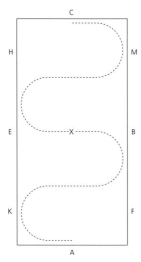

NOVICE – walk .

INTERMEDIATE – walk, trot.

ADVANCED – walk, trot, canter (with a change of lead through trot or walk each time the centre line is crossed).

EXERCISE 93 – HALF TURN ABOUT OR ON THE FOREHAND

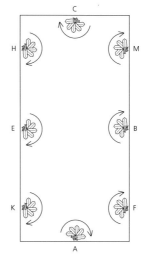

NOVICE – walk – turn about.

INTERMEDIATE – halt – turn on.

ADVANCED – halt – turn on.

PROBLEMS, Exercises 84–93

- Loss of balance, rhythm and impulsion during the turns.
- Lack of straightness.
- Lack of bend.
- Inaccurate use of the letters.
- Loss of shape and size of the half circles.

7 LENGTHENING AND SHORTENING

Lengthening and shortening teaches the rider that the horse has variety within his paces, and should also improve the horse's way of going. The rider's ability to lengthen and shorten the stride clarifies 'feel' for the horse's working paces, and therefore aids an understanding of the horse's correct way of going. Riders who are able to vary the horse's length of stride should be able to utilise this skill when jumping.

BEGINNER

Lengthening and shortening the stride really starts at novice level, but even beginners have some control of the paces, and can feel when they succeed in making them bigger or smaller.

NOVICE

Once novice riders can maintain a consistent contact, and have a relatively balanced and secure position, they can start to work towards varying the pace. Counting strides helps to reinforce a feel for shortening and lengthening the stride as it will illustrate the fact that the horse takes more or fewer strides to cover a set distance, for example, down the long side of the school.

Exercises should remain basic, with the instructor focusing on maintenance of the rider's position at all times. The novice rider can be introduced to the theory of the four different types of walk, trot and canter.

The variation in pace must be explained so that the riders understand that the stride shortens due to the step becoming higher, and that the lengthening comes from allowing forward the energy which was created during the shortening. This theory will need to be repeated at intermediate and advanced levels.

INTERMEDIATE

The aims are to further develop co-ordination between leg and hand, and to achieve greater balance and more accurate transitions within the pace. Maintaining rhythm throughout should be emphasised at this level. A good intermediate should be able to start varying the length of the canter.

ADVANCED

Advanced riders should be able to produce clearer transitions and a higher quality of work, maintaining the horse's balance and rhythm. Their position should be secure throughout the work.

The easiest pace to work with initially is the trot. Try to avoid doing much in the walk, as it is easy to lose the quality of the pace; and canter obviously requires a more experienced rider.

AIMS AND BENEFITS

RIDER
- Co-ordination.
- Accuracy.

- Feel.
- Position.

HORSE

- Balance.
- Rhythm.
- Suppleness.
- Straightness.
- Impulsion.
- Engagement.

LENGTHENING AND SHORTENING IN THE TROT

1. SIMPLE SHORTENING AND LENGTHENING

RIDER LEVEL Good beginners (almost novice).

AIMS AND BENEFITS

- To develop the rider's awareness of the horse's capacity for showing variety within the pace.

EXERCISE 94

- With the ride halted along one long side, lead file in succession trot to the rear of the ride, making the trot 'smaller' and 'bigger' between specific letters.

- Encourage the riders to use their legs and hands correctly.

EXERCISE 95

- As above, with the ride in walk going large.

EXERCISE 96

- Make the stride shorter and longer as a ride together (if the riders are at the stage where they are capable of trotting together safely).

PROBLEMS, Exercises 94–96

- Co-ordination of the aids.
- Loss of rhythm (at this level, this is to be expected. The exercise purely shows beginners that they can influence the horse.)

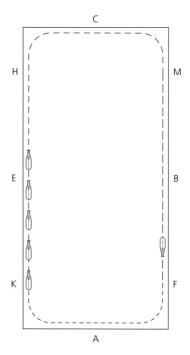

EXERCISES 94–96

2. SIMPLE SHORTENING AND LENGTHENING IN OPEN ORDER GOING LARGE OR ON 20M CIRCLES

RIDER LEVEL Novice and intermediate.

AIMS AND BENEFITS

- Builds the rider's ability to vary the pace.

EXERCISES 97–99

- Encourage the rider to maintain the rhythm.

EXERCISE 97

- In walk and trot, ride go large, working to maintain balance and rhythm.

EXERCISE 98

- In trot, progressively shorten the stride on the short sides of the school and lengthen on the long sides.

EXERCISE 99

- Shorten the trot along one long side and lengthen along the opposite side.

- Count the number of strides on each long side and compare.

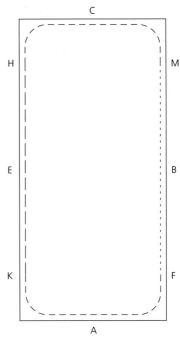

EXERCISES 97–99

PROBLEMS, Exercises 96–98

- Co-ordination of the aids.
- Working the horse between leg and hand.
- Most riders tend to put more effort into lengthening than shortening, simply because it is easier to feel something 'happen'. Riders need to be aware that the amount lengthened has a direct relationship to the energy created through shortening.
- Rider does not use the leg when shortening the stride.
- Rider loses contact on the reins during lengthening. This allows the horse to fall on the forehand. Contain the energy between leg and hand.

EXERCISE 100

- The above exercises can be ridden on 20m circles, dividing each circle in half for shortening and lengthening.

PROBLEMS

- The rider must work hard to maintain the shape of the circle.

NOTE: If canter has been used in the warm up, canter again at the end of the lesson. Riders should feel that the quality of the canter has improved due to improved impulsion, engagement, and the horses becoming more forward thinking.

3. MORE DEMANDING EXERCISES FOR SHORTENING AND LENGTHENING

RIDER LEVEL Advanced.

AIMS AND BENEFITS

- To produce clearer and more accurate transitions, working towards medium and collected trot.

EXERCISE 101

- Use 10m, 15m and 20m circles to aid riders to achieve shortening and lengthening.

- Spiral in and out of a 20m circle at A or C.

- 10m shortened trot.

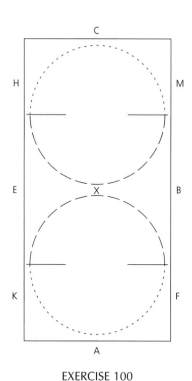

EXERCISE 100

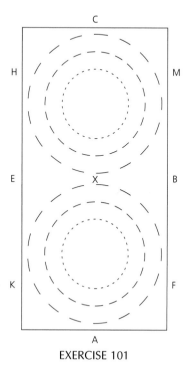

EXERCISE 101

- 15m working trot.

- 20m lengthened trot.

PROBLEMS

- As riders begin to develop a feel for shortening and lengthening, they often start to become tense as they ask for the shortening. They must learn to work with the horse.
- Riders do not maintain the shape or size of the circles.

EXERCISE 102

- Go large in trot in open order.

- Lengthen on the long sides and shorten on the short sides.

- Ride a 10m circle at the end of each long side, which should help the rider to shorten the horse more accurately, thus developing a clearer transition.

PROBLEMS

- This can lead to abrupt, unbalanced transitions if not ridden correctly as riders commence the 10m circle.

EXERCISE 103

- Riders trot in open order on 20m circles.

- Develop control and feel by asking for four working trot steps, then four collected steps, and then four medium steps. Repeat.

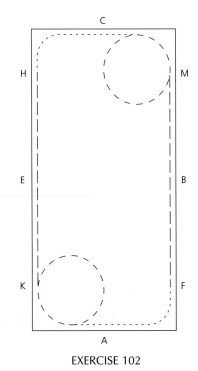

EXERCISE 102

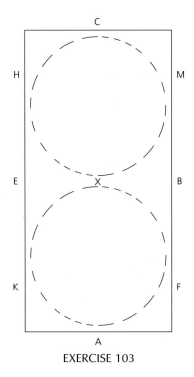

EXERCISE 103

PROBLEMS

- This is demanding of horse and rider. Do not ride for too long.
- The exercise requires a high level of co-ordination of the aids and preparation.

LENGTHENING AND SHORTENING IN THE CANTER

RIDER LEVEL Good intermediate and advanced.

AIMS AND BENEFITS
- To introduce the work into the canter.

EXERCISE 104

- Divide the ride onto two 20m circles.

- One or two riders at a time, ask them to ride three circles in canter:

  – circle 1 working canter,

  – circle 2 shortened canter,

  – circle 3 lengthened canter.

- Count the number of strides on each circle.

PROBLEMS

- Loss of balance and rhythm in the canter.
- Tension of horse and rider.

EXERCISE 105

- This exercise is similar to exercise 100, except that it is performed in canter.

- Divide the ride onto two circles, and work one or two riders at a time.

- Riders divide the circle in two and ride one half shortened, the other half lengthened.

- Count the strides on each half of the circle.

PROBLEMS

- Loss of balance and rhythm in the canter due to the rider trying to achieve good results.
- Lack of preparation for the transition.

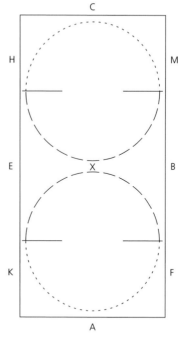

EXERCISE 105

EXERCISE 106

- For advanced groups, start to ask for the transitions to be quicker and more accurate, e.g. medium canter KEH, working canter at H, trot at C.

PROBLEMS

- Loss of balance and rhythm in the canter.
- Tension of horse and rider.
- Horse is allowed to fall on the forehand.
- Horse is not ridden between leg and hand, and breaks into trot.

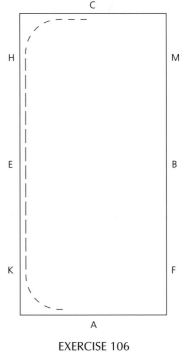

EXERCISE 106

8 LATERAL WORK

Lateral work takes riding into a new dimension. It is enjoyable to teach and helps riders to develop feel and co-ordination. Lateral work helps to improve the horse's way of going by creating engagement of the hindquarters.

BEGINNER

Lateral work is not suitable for beginners.

NOVICE

The term 'novice' spans a wide range of abilities. An inexperienced novice is able to become familiar with the areas of the school where lateral work is ridden, such as the three-quarter line, which is a valuable lesson in itself, but may not actually have the co-ordination to leg yield. A more experienced novice should be starting to co-ordinate the aids needed to leg yield and ride turns about the forehand.

INTERMEDIATE

Intermediate riders further develop their feel and co-ordination of the aids to 'feel' the theory learned at novice level. The exercises need to increase in difficulty gradually in order to improve ability. It is also valuable to make the exercises easier again occasionally, at which point riders often find that the feeling of riding the horse between leg and hand 'clicks', as they are suddenly able to ride the easier exercises more accurately. This then gives riders a 'feel' to try to achieve in the more complex exercises.

ADVANCED

Advanced riders should be concerned with correct application of the aids and the horse's correct way of going. They should strive to maintain the horse's rhythm, balance, straightness, impulsion and suppleness and their own position and, in doing so, use the exercises to improve the horse's way of going.

AIMS AND BENEFITS

RIDER
- Co-ordination and application of the aids.
- Riding the horse between leg and hand.
- Position.

HORSE
- Balance.
- Rhythm.
- Impulsion.
- Straightness.
- Suppleness.
- Engagement.

LEG YIELDING

1. FOUNDATION FOR LEG YIELDING (THREE-QUARTER LINE)

RIDER LEVEL Inexperienced novices.

AIMS AND BENEFITS
- Foundation for lateral work on the three-quarter line, keeping the horse straight without the support of the boards.

EXERCISE 107

- Mark out the two three-quarter lines in the school by using a cone in each corner.

- Walk both three-quarter lines continuously as a ride. Explain that riding good corners and keeping the horse straight is essential.

- Lead file in succession trot to the rear of the ride.

- Trot as a ride on the three-quarter lines.

PROBLEMS
- Poor corners and lack of straightness due to a lack of co-ordination of the aids.

EXERCISE 108

- With the ride in trot on the three-quarter lines, rear file in succession makes a transition to walk.

- As the ride catches up, the rider in walk makes a transition to trot as the lead file.

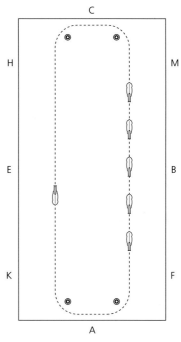

EXERCISES 107 and 108

PROBLEMS
- When at the front of the ride, some horses will have a tendency to drift towards the track.

2. FOUNDATION FOR LEG YIELDING (15M AND 20M CIRCLES)

RIDER LEVEL Inexperienced novices.

AIMS AND BENEFITS
- Foundation work for leg yielding out and spiralling in on a circle.

EXERCISE 109

- With the whole ride on one 20m circle, teach the ride how to ride a 15m circle within the 20m circle.

- Firstly in walk and then in trot, spiral in and out of the circles, between 15 and 20m.

- The ride could then be split onto two 20m circles at A and C, and the exercise repeated.

PROBLEMS

- Lack of spatial awareness, and therefore lack of accuracy.
- Horses fall out or in on the 15m circle due to lack of co-ordination of the aids.

3. EARLY LEG YIELDING

RIDER LEVEL Good novice.

AIMS AND BENEFITS
- Introduction to leg yielding.

EXERCISE 110

- Having refreshed the riders' memories regarding riding good corners and straight three-quarter lines, halt the ride and give an explanation and possibly a demonstration of leg yielding.

- Set the ride off in walk, in open or closed order, taking the three-quarter line on both sides of the school and leg yielding towards the track.

- Offer individual help.

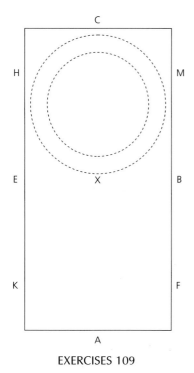

EXERCISES 109

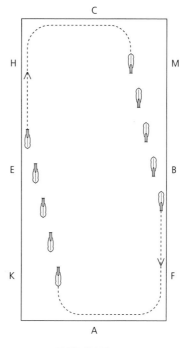

EXERCISES 110

- Repeat the exercise in trot – to aid the horse and rider in the leg yield and to add variety, a 15m circle could be included at the A and C ends of the school.

PROBLEMS

- Loss of position. This is an area to which the instructor must pay particular attention.
- Horse falls through the outside shoulder. Correct, but do not make riders lose confidence over this. As the co-ordination of the aids improves, so will this aspect of the work
- Rider concentrates on the leg yielding more than the corner. From the outset, the instructor must advise that 'everything comes out of a corner'. The corner must be ridden to the best of the rider's ability.

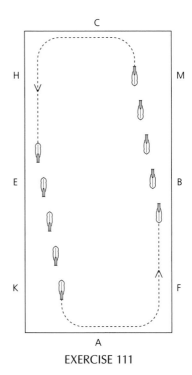

EXERCISE 111

4. DEVELOPING LEG YIELDING EXERCISES

RIDER LEVEL Intermediate and advanced.

AIMS AND BENEFITS

- More complex exercises to develop leg to hand co-ordination and feel for leg yielding.

EXERCISE 111

- Leg yield from an inner track towards the three-quarter line. (Starting from an inner track means that the horses are not 'stuck' to the boards.)

PROBLEMS

- It is harder to move the horse away from the boards.
- Likely to lose straightness, balance and rhythm and rider's position.

EXERCISE 112

- Leg yield from the three-quarter line, aiming to reach an inner track opposite E or B, at which point the rider leg yields back towards the three-quarter line.

PROBLEMS

- Riders need to be made aware that there must be a few steps of straightness and then a change of

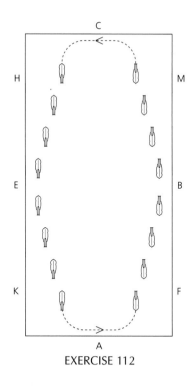

EXERCISE 112

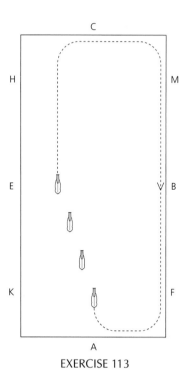

EXERCISE 113

bend for the horse to be able to change the direction of leg yielding.

- Again, moving away from the boards is more difficult and likely to cause a loss of balance and rhythm.

EXERCISE 113

- Leg yield from the centre line towards the three-quarter line.

PROBLEMS

- Leg yielding from the centre line is more challenging, as the boards offer no support and the horse has to be entirely guided and balanced by the rider.
- It is not practicable to ride this exercise on both sides of the school, as the rider would need to turn a half 5m circle from the three-quarter line to the centre line.

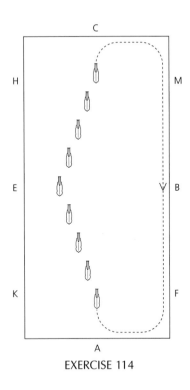

EXERCISE 114

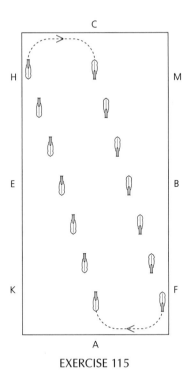

EXERCISE 115

EXERCISE 114

- Leg yield from the centre line to the three-quarter line and back towards the centre line again.

PROBLEMS

- As exercise 112.

EXERCISE 115

- Leg yield from the centre line to the track.

PROBLEMS

- The greater distance to cover implies that the leg yielding steps must cover more ground laterally. Riders must work to maintain the forward-thinking energy at the same time, or loss of balance, rhythm and straightness will occur. Do not let the riders believe that reaching the track is the priority, or the quality of the work will be lost.

EXERCISE 116

- On the centre line or three-quarter line, leg yield zig-zags three steps left, three steps straight, three steps right, three steps straight. Repeat.

PROBLEMS

- A very demanding exercise that requires lots of preparation, accuracy, co-ordination of the aids and feel. When ridden well, it should greatly improve the horse's way of going.

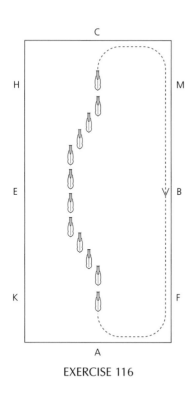

EXERCISE 116

EXERCISE 117

- With the ride in open order, begin leg yielding through the first gap between the poles towards the track.

EXERCISE 118

- Once this is achieved, leg yield from the outside of the second pole through the gap to the inside of the third pole.

EXERCISE 119

- Combine the two above exercises so that the riders are 'zig-zagging' in and out of the poles.

5. LEG YIELDING USING POLES

RIDER LEVEL Intermediate and advanced.

AIMS AND BENEFITS
- Adds variety and precision.

EXERCISES 117–120

- Lay out three poles on both three-quarter lines, an equal distance apart.

- Develop the exercises, firstly in walk, and then in trot.

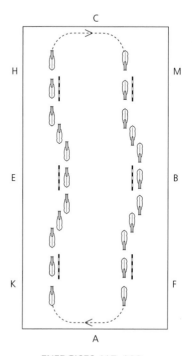

EXERCISES 117–120

EXERCISE 120

- The above exercise can be reversed so that the riders start on the outside of the first pole.

PROBLEMS, Exercises 117–120

- There is always a minor safety issue when using poles. Ensure that riders know that their horses must not touch the poles. As an alternative, cones could be used instead.
- All exercises are surprisingly good at encouraging precision, and usually produce excellent results.
- Insist on rider straightness.

6. LEG YIELDING ON A CIRCLE

RIDER LEVEL Intermediate and advanced.

AIMS AND BENEFITS

- When ridden accurately, leg yielding on a circle offers a greater feel of the horse stepping under itself.

EXERCISE 121

- With the ride divided onto two 20m circles at A and C in open order, riders are to leg yield in and spiral out on the circle between 10m, 15m and 20m.

- This exercise is most productive if the instructor gives commands for when the riders should leg yield, rather than leaving the riders to do it themselves.

- The instructor can vary the time allowed for the ride to leg yield onto a different size circle, e.g. in

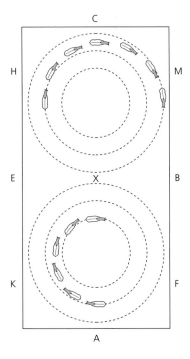

EXERCISE 121

the distance of a quarter of a circle, riders are to leg yield out from 15 to 20m. (A longer distance would be easier for riders of lower ability.)

- Repeat on both reins in walk and trot.

PROBLEMS

- During leg yielding on a circle it is potentially easier for the horse to fall through the outside shoulder than on a straight line. Offer the riders the advice that they need to think of pushing the quarters of the horse over first. This inevitably will not happen, but if it does, it will require correction. Usually, with the thought of moving the quarters first, the rider tends to use the outside leg more to prevent the shoulders from falling out, and a better quality of leg yielding is achieved, as the horse remains straighter.

7. CANTER EXERCISES DEVELOPED FROM LEG YIELDING

RIDER LEVEL Intermediate and advanced.

AIMS AND BENEFITS

• Variety, transitions to canter on a straight line, aided by leg yielding.

EXERCISE 122

• In ride order, the ride turns up the three-quarter line and leg yields towards the track.

• Lead file, on reaching the track, makes a transition to canter and canters large to the rear of the ride.

• The rest of the ride can remain in trot, or make a transition to walk before the lead file canters, depending on ability, weather conditions and horses' temperaments.

PROBLEMS

• Preparation for the canter transition must be ridden during the leg yielding in order for the transition to be made as the rider reaches the track.

• If the horse strikes off on the incorrect lead, return to trot and ask again in the next corner.

EXERCISE 123 (ADVANCED)

• In ride order, ride leg yields from the three-quarter line towards the centre line, aiming to reach the centre line at X.

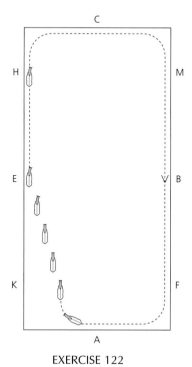

EXERCISE 122

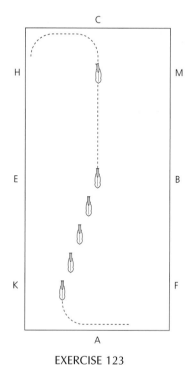

EXERCISE 123

- Lead file makes a transition to canter at X, aiming for a named lead leg, and canters in the direction of the lead leg to the rear of the ride. (If leg yielding left to right, ask for left canter and vice versa.)

- The rest of the ride can remain in trot, or make a transition to walk, before the lead file canters. At C track in the direction of the lead file.

PROBLEMS

- Possible loss of straightness during the leg yielding, which will lead to a loss of balance during the canter transition.
- Lack of preparation time can cause riders to rush the canter transition.
- The turn at C onto the track must be ridden well.
- Riders should not turn up the centre line in canter, as the canter may have become long and flat along the long side.

TURN ON THE FOREHAND

1. TURN ABOUT THE FOREHAND

RIDER LEVEL Good novice.

AIMS AND BENEFITS
- An introduction to lateral work, foundation work for turn on the forehand.

EXERCISE 124

- Place a block or cone on an inner track in the four corners of the school.

- Explain the aids for turn about the forehand and the difference from turn on the forehand.

- With the ride in walk in open order on an inner track, ride a turn about the forehand at each cone.

- Provide the horses and riders with frequent changes of rein and periods of trot to keep both horses and riders thinking forwards.

PROBLEMS

- Horses lose forwardness – periods of trot should prevent this.
- Rider turns the horse with the rein rather than the leg.
- Loss of position.

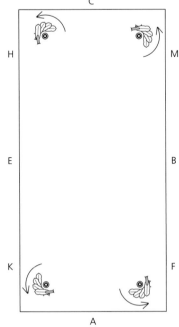

EXERCISE 124

2. TURN ON THE FOREHAND

RIDER LEVEL Intermediate and advanced.

AIMS AND BENEFITS

- CO-ORDINATION OF THE AIDS.
- Improvement in the canter.

EXERCISE 125

- With the ride in walk in open order on an inner track, halt in front of the boards of the school, and ride a quarter turn on the forehand.

- Each time the rider reaches E or B, trot a 15m circle, and then continue the exercise at the other end of the school in walk. (Advanced riders could develop this to riding a 15m circle in canter, before resuming the exercise.)

PROBLEMS

- Loss of position.
- Rider uses the rein to turn the horse, which results in the horse walking forwards.

EXERCISE 126

- As exercise 125, but this time making a quarter turn on the forehand at a cone placed on an inner track in the four corners of the school. This is more difficult, as the wall will have helped to maintain the halt.

PROBLEMS

- As exercise 125.
- The halt is not maintained, and the horse walks forwards.

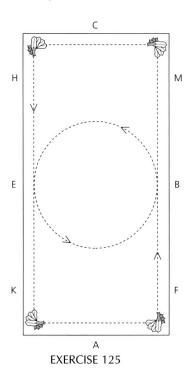

EXERCISE 125

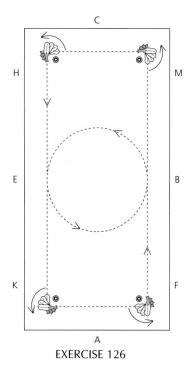

EXERCISE 126

9 WORK WITHOUT STIRRUPS OR REINS

WORK WITHOUT STIRRUPS

Working without stirrups is highly beneficial for all
levels. It improves balance and position, deepens
the seat, lengthens the leg and develops 'feel'. The
instructor's aim is to teach riders how to sit lightly to
the trot and canter, and improve the rider's position
and balance. It is important to monitor rider fitness
levels so that the experience is not uncomfortable.

SUPPLING AND POSITIONAL EXERCISES

EXERCISE 127 – SCISSOR LEGS

- Riders swing opposite legs backwards and
  forwards, from the hip rather from the knee.

- This helps to deepen the seat, lengthen the leg, and
  put the whole leg into a more correct position.

EXERCISE 128 – JOCKEY KNEES

- Working with alternate legs, riders lift one knee up
  to the pommel of the saddle, then lift the knee out
  to the side, and then push it back and down into
  its correct position.

- This helps to open the hips and knees and bring
  the leg into a more correct position.

EXERCISE 129 – CIRCLING THE FEET

- Working with both feet together, riders circle their
  feet first one way, and then the other.

- This helps to relax the ankle joint and the calf
  muscles.

EXERCISE 130 – BRINGING THE HEEL TO THE BASE OF THE SEAT

- Working with one leg at a time, riders place both
  reins and the whip into the outside hand. (Ensure
  that the outside rein is slightly shorter to prevent
  the horses from turning into the middle of the
  school.) Using their inside hand, the riders can
  pull their inside heel up to the base of their seat.
  (Watch that they do not catch the horse's loins
  with their toes.) Now ask them to move their knee
  towards the horse's tail, without tipping forwards
  as they do so. Gently release the lower leg back
  into position, without losing the position of the
  thigh. Repeat with the other leg.

- This encourages the leg to hang in a more correct

position and generally results in the rider sitting up taller.

Watch how each rider performs these exercises, as weaknesses in the position generally come from tightness within the physique.

THE BASIC POSITION

For flatwork, the correct basic position should have a straight vertical line – ear, shoulder, hip and heel. A straight line should also run from the elbow, through a straight wrist and hand, down the rein to the bit. Initially, encourage the hands to remain hip-width apart. This helps the rider to develop the feel of riding from leg to hand. Later, when the rider is more established, the hands can become closer.

There are various reasons why riders will fail to maintain this position during a lesson:
- lack of suppleness,
- lack of fitness,
- misuse of strength,
- shape of the rider,
- shape of the horse,
- the influence of the saddle over the way the rider sits,
- attitude to riding – tense, nervous, relaxed,
- determination to improve, discipline and focus.

To improve the rider, the teacher needs to understand the root cause of the positional weakness, such as nervousness, and address this before insisting on positional accuracy.

Improvement in the rider's ability comes as a package, including security of position, correct aid application, feel and confidence.

TEACHING SITTING TROT

In order that riders can remain in balance with the horse and give the illusion of sitting still when in trot or canter, the instructor needs to explain how to absorb the movement of the horse through the hips, seat and lower back.

It is important in the beginning that riders are not over-faced with a horse having a big movement. Ideally you want a rhythmical horse, with a gentle movement, that will stoically accept the rider learning the sitting trot.

Riders should make the inside rein longer, and hold the front of the saddle with the inside hand, not as if they were going on a white knuckle ride, but with their fingertips under the front of the saddle, gently pulling them deeper into the saddle. The outside rein can then control the speed and keep them out on the track.

Initially, riders should be encouraged to sit back on their seat bones, with their shoulders slightly behind their hips and their lower legs wrapped around the horse's sides. (At this moment you may have slightly sacrificed their position in order that they can feel and absorb the movement of the horse. Once they can do this, it is relatively easy to encourage them to sit upright again.)

Explain that the lower back and hips need to move slightly in order to absorb the horse's movement in trot. Most importantly, the riders must stay relaxed!

In the beginning, ask for short periods of trot, e.g. down the long side of the school. Remember it is demanding work. Try not to do too much too early. If the rider cannot walk for the next week, the instructor has failed to assess the rider's level of fitness and suppleness correctly!

BEGINNER

Beginner riders should be able to ride suppling exercises in the halt and walk. Teach them how to take away stirrups correctly and how to retake them afterwards, encouraging them to find their stirrups without looking.

NOVICE

Pay special attention to teaching the novice rider how to absorb the movement correctly from the outset. Short periods of trot are more beneficial than longer periods. Riders are aiming to improve their position and balance, which begins with them being able to absorb the movement. Riders should work towards being able to identify the steps taken by the horse's hind legs in the walk.

INTERMEDIATE

Intermediate riders should be able to absorb the movement sufficiently well that the instructor can make achievable positional corrections and develop security. They should work towards being able to go from rising trot to sitting trot without affecting the rhythm or balance of the horse. Riders can start to develop the feel of the horse's hind leg steps in the trot, and they can start to ride easy canter exercises without stirrups.

ADVANCED

Advanced riders should aim to maintain a balanced, supple and accurate position without stirrups in walk, trot and canter. They should be able to influence the horse better during transitions and lateral work, by having a good feel for the horse's hind leg steps. They should start to be aware of the influence of their weight aids, and work to be in harmony with the horse at all times, while developing a deeper seat, a longer length of leg and a secure lower leg.

EXERCISES FOR WORK WITHOUT STIRRUPS

1. EXERCISES IN HALT AND WALK

RIDER LEVEL Tiny tots, beginners using leaders as necessary (plus novice to advanced riders warm-up).

AIMS AND BENEFITS
- Confidence.
- Balance.
- Position.
- Suppleness.

EXERCISE 131

- In halt, ride quit and cross stirrups correctly.

- Either in halt with lead file in succession, or as a ride in walk, take the ride through the positional exercises listed above.

- Play 'Simon Says' (young children). See Chapter 14, Games and Obstacle Courses.

PROBLEMS
- Exercises not performed correctly, and therefore not as beneficial as they could be.
- Cramp in the hips, from tension. Turn in and halt, and if necessary dismount until it has passed.

2. STARTING TO TROT WITHOUT STIRRUPS

RIDER LEVEL Novice.

AIMS AND BENEFITS
- Balance.
- Feel.
- Absorption of the movement.

EXERCISES 132–136

- Explain to the riders how they must hold the saddle at first, using the inside hand.

- Explain how to sit to the trot.

EXERCISE 132

- With the ride in halt, lead file in succession trot a long side of the school. (At first, especially with children, the instructor may need to run with the pony to maintain the same rhythm, and may also need to hold the rider's inside ankle to aid balance.)

EXERCISE 133

- As above, without a leader. In this situation, a faster horse or pony can be kept slow by setting the riders off two at a time, using a slower pony in front to set the pace, as long as the ponies are friendly!

EXERCISE 134

- With the ride walking large, lead file in succession trot large to the rear of the ride. This can be repeated, two riders at a time.

EXERCISE 135

- Gradually build up the number of riders trotting together until the whole ride is able safely to do sitting trot going large around the school, maintaining their distances. (This may take several lessons.)

EXERCISE 136

- The group can now begin to trot simple school figures as a ride. Gradually build up the length of time that riders are in sitting trot.

- By this stage, most of the group should be beginning to let go of the saddle with the inside hand. Encourage the elbows and shoulders to remain relaxed to prevent the hands from moving.

PROBLEMS, Exercises 131–136
- Safety is always the main priority. Reaching Exercise 136 can take many weeks, and cannot be rushed.
- Notice rider fitness levels and do not over-stress.
- Gripping with the knees.
- Tension within the position, leading to stitches. Allow frequent rests.

A useful exercise to introduce now is to ask the ride to do rising trot without their stirrups. This teaches riders to feel when the horse is pushing them out of the saddle, rather than rising robotically.

3. DEVELOPING FEEL FOR THE HIND LEG STEPS

RIDER LEVEL Novice, intermediate and advanced.

AIMS AND BENEFITS
- Develops feel for the hind leg steps.

EXERCISE 137 (NOVICE)

- With the ride in walk, going large, ask the riders if they can feel the side-to-side movement of their hips as the horses walk.

- Refine this feeling by asking if they can sense that as one hip is taken up and forwards, the other is let back and down, as if their seat is walking.

- Ask the riders to concentrate on their inside hip. The inside hip is moved by the horse's inside hind leg. When the hind leg is on the ground, the hip comes up; when the horse's hind leg is in the air, the hip goes down.

- While in walk, ask the riders individually to identify when the horse's inside hind leg is on the ground, which is when their inside hip comes up.

- Even at this level, novice riders should be encouraged to use their legs in the rhythm of the pace. Discover if the riders can encourage the horses to take bigger walk steps by using their legs alternately, as the horse's hind leg is in the air.

PROBLEMS
- Riders say they cannot feel any difference in their hips. Tell them to relax the seat, and then identify for them when the horse's inside hind leg is on the ground. Usually, they can then continue to feel it.
- Riders feel the rhythm and then switch off to it, resulting in them not feeling when there is a change in rhythm, for example, around the corners.

EXERCISE 138 (INTERMEDIATE AND ADVANCED)

- The previous exercise can be developed for intermediate and advanced riders by taking it into the trot.

- Once the feel is established in the walk, the rider should try to feel the same thing in the trot. Keep the exercise simple by keeping the ride going large, either in ride order or open order.

PROBLEMS
- Riders find it difficult to carry what they can feel in the walk over into the trot. Tell the riders to relax their seat and hold the pommel of the saddle to draw them deeper into the saddle. Usually riders start to feel the movement. If not, call the movement out as they trot. This may also help.

IMPLICATIONS OF THIS EXERCISE
- The rider can identify the correct diagonal from feel rather than looking. As the inside hip comes up, the rider should be sitting; as the outside hip comes up, or the inside hip goes down, the rider should be rising. Practise.

- The aid for the canter can be given more positively at the right moment. The moment for the aid for canter is as the inside hip comes up. This is when the outside hind leg is in the air and can start the first beat of canter. Practise.

- Aids given during lateral work can be made more effective if the rider can give the aid as the inside hind leg is in the air, encouraging the horse to step further underneath itself and develop greater impulsion.

When starting to work in open order without stirrups, keep the work simple. Until advanced level, work without stirrups may need to be of a slightly lower level than the riders' work with stirrups.

Advanced riders should be able to ride all exercises equally, with or without stirrups.

For canter exercises for intermediate and advanced riders, see Chapter 10, Canter Exercises. Start with the most basic exercises and work up through the levels of difficulty. Never force anyone to canter without stirrups.

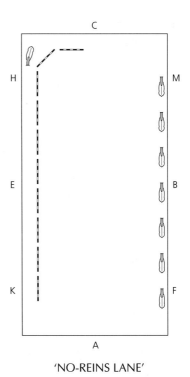

'NO-REINS LANE'

WORK WITHOUT REINS

Work without reins develops balance and confidence at all levels. Most horses and ponies are very accepting of the exercises used, but must be trained initially. Time of year and weather conditions will dictate whether safety may be a reason to leave this theme for a more appropriate week.
The no-rein lane is set up very much like a jumping lane to ensure that the horses remain on the track for the period of time that the riders are without reins. Set it up along one long side of the school, including the previous corner, e.g. from C to K. Halt the ride on the opposite side of the school, facing C, with knots in their reins. They must come through

one at a time, and only let go of their reins for the time that they are in the no-rein lane.

BEGINNER

Initially, working without reins is a daunting prospect for any beginner. Ensure that you are confident in the horses and ponies. Beginners can ride exercises in the walk, with the possibility of developing a little trot work. This should greatly develop confidence and it is lovely to see apprehension replaced with enjoyment when the riders find it simple.

NOVICE

The novice should be able to ride all of the exercises in walk and trot, including downward transitions from trot to walk. Work to improve balance, suppleness and position.

INTERMEDIATE

The intermediate rider should be able to ride the exercises in walk, trot and canter. They should start to become aware of the importance of their upper body in relation to the downward transitions, and therefore further develop their feel for riding a more balanced transition.

ADVANCED

The advanced rider should use the exercises to confirm a good basic position, improve suppleness and further develop feel, timing and balance during downwards transitions.

EXERCISES FOR WORK WITHOUT REINS

EXERCISE 139 – WINDMILL

Starting with one arm pointing down and one up, rotate the arms in backward circles like backstroke. Move the arms in the rhythm of the walk, trot and canter.

* This helps riders to grow taller and bring their shoulders back.

NOTE: When starting to windmill in the canter, the exercise can be started gradually by the rider holding onto the saddle with the inside hand and doing the windmill with the outside arm only.

EXERCISE 140 – TWISTER

With the arms held straight out to the side, twist the upper body towards the centre of the school and then to the outside. Repeat. Move the arms in the rhythm of the walk, trot and canter.

* The exercise helps to supple riders at the waist.

EXERCISE 141 – ARMS IN FRONT

Hold the arms straight out in front of the body.

* Improves balance.

EXERCISE	BEGINNER	NOVICE	INTERMEDIATE/ADVANCED
WINDMILL	Walk	Walk, trot	Walk, trot, canter
TWISTER	Walk	Walk, trot	Walk, trot, canter
ARMS IN FRONT	Walk	Walk, trot	Walk, trot, canter
REIN POSITION	Walk	Walk, trot, canter	Walk, trot, canter
RUB STOMACH	Walk	Walk, trot	Walk, trot, canter
STANDING UP	Walk	Walk, trot	Walk, trot, canter (advanced)
BALANCED POSITION	Walk	Walk, trot	Walk, trot, canter

EXERCISE 142 – REIN POSITION

Hold the hands in the rein position. A whip can be placed on the rider's wrists to focus the rider on maintaining the position.

• Valuable for improving the position of the hands.

EXERCISE 143 – RUB STOMACH AND PAT HEAD AT THE SAME TIME

Rub the stomach with one hand and pat head with the other at the same time. Swap over hands halfway through the lane.

• A great co-ordination exercise.

EXERCISE 144 – STANDING UP

Stand up straight with the arms out straight in front. Find the point of balance.

• Helps to improve the rider's balance.

EXERCISE 145 – BALANCED POSITION

Take balanced position with the arms straight out behind.

• Improves balance and softness through the knees and ankles.

WITHOUT REINS GAMES

Children appreciate these games.

1. HEAD, SHOULDERS, KNEES AND TOES

As the title suggests, the riders are going to touch their heads, shoulders, knees and toes.

2. SIMON SAYS

See Chapter 14, Games and Obstacle Courses.

3. THE ANIMAL GAME

You need a confident group to do this. Ask them to think of their favourite animal. As they walk or trot through the no-rein lane, they will make the noise and actions of their favourite animal. The rest of the group can guess what the animal is. If some are shy, the instructor could make the noises while they do the actions!

4. MAKE UP OWN EXERCISE

Each rider can make up his or her own exercise to do through the lane, and explain the benefit of the exercise, e.g. suppleness, balance, co-ordination. Some may need a little help.

TRANSITIONS WITHOUT REINS

Generally, school horses will make downward transitions naturally as they come to the rear of the ride. As a result, the letter at which the downward transitions are asked for will determine the level of difficulty of the exercise. E.g. a transition from trot to walk at K, nearer to the rear of the ride, will be easier than at B.

As a guide, novices should be able to make a downward transition from trot to walk at K, intermediates and advanced at B. Canter to trot for the intermediates could be at K, and advanced at B.

AIDS FOR THE DOWNWARD TRANSITIONS
Focus on the influence of the upper body while maintaining leg position.

TROT TO WALK
Slow the rising, take sitting trot, and grow tall with the upper body. Keep the leg on.

CANTER TO TROT
Grow tall and cease moving with the hips. Keep the leg on.

10 CANTER EXERCISES

The canter has a three-beat rhythm. When teaching riders, the canter is usually the weak link in their work, mainly because it is the pace in which least work is done. As riders develop confidence and feel for riding the canter, combined with security of position and co-ordination of the aids, the canter work tends to improve quickly.

BEGINNER
Beginners will not learn the canter at this stage of their training.

NOVICE
When introducing canter to novice riders it is important that they learn on suitable horses and ponies. The horses should have a comfortable canter and maintain a relatively slow rhythm, kept by the instructor.

As the ability to maintain the position in the canter and during the transitions improves, riders can be taught how to ask for the transitions to and from canter themselves.

INTERMEDIATE
Intermediate riders are often keen to develop their canter skills. The aim of the instructor should be to keep the exercises in canter varied, but fairly basic, in order to give the riders the opportunity to improve the basic skills required. Security of position, feel and co-ordination of the aids all need to develop at this stage in order for the rider to perform the more difficult exercises expected at advanced level.

ADVANCED
Advanced riders require exercises that challenge them in the canter, in order to start to ride and improve the canter as opposed to simply maintaining it, as at intermediate level. As the exercises increase in difficulty, so the riders' position may deteriorate as they rise to the challenge. Positional corrections are essential.

AIMS AND BENEFITS

RIDER
- Position and balance.
- Co-ordination of the aids.
- Feel.

HORSE
- Balance.
- Rhythm.
- Impulsion.
- Engagement.
- Straightness.
- Suppleness.
- Fitness.

GOING LARGE

1. RIDE IN HALT, LEAD FILE CANTERS TO THE REAR OF THE RIDE

For details of this exercise see Chapter 3, Transitions, Canter Exercises in Closed Order, Exercise 7 (page 18).

2. RIDE IN HALT, LEAD FILE MAKES A TRANSITION TO CANTER AT X ON A 20M CIRCLE

For details of this exercise see Chapter 3, Transitions, Canter Exercises in Closed Order, Exercise 8 (page 19).

Continue using these two exercises as advised in Chapter 3.

3. RIDE IN WALK OR TROT, LEAD FILE CANTERS TO THE REAR OF THE RIDE

For details of this exercise see Chapter 3, Transitions, Canter Exercises in Closed Order, Exercise 9 (page 20).

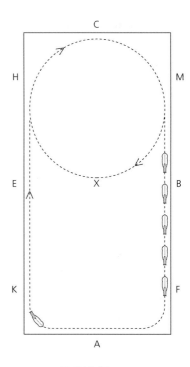

EXERCISE 146

EXERCISE 146

- Ridden as exercise 9, including riding a 20m circle at the 'free' end of the school before cantering to the rear of the ride.

PROBLEMS
- Across the different levels you will expect different levels of accuracy of the circle. The first time a novice rider rides a 20m circle in canter it may not be the perfect shape or size, but should improve relatively quickly. If you have spent time initially developing the rider's balance and seat in the canter, you will usually find that the rider will pleasantly surprise you!
- Many horses will become long and flat along the

long sides in the canter and may fall into trot if not corrected.

- The 20m circle usually helps to connect the canter again, partly because of the shape and partly because the circle will be the rider's focus and they will therefore ride it more strongly. The rider then often takes a 'breather' having achieved the circle, which is when the horse will fall into trot. Explain this to the riders and encourage them to keep riding the canter between leg and hand at all times.

Exercises 9 and 146 could be ridden keeping the rest of the ride in trot, depending on rider ability, weather conditions and horses' temperaments. Alternatively, walk the ride for the lead file's transition to canter, and once the lead file is two letters ahead, the ride can resume the trot.

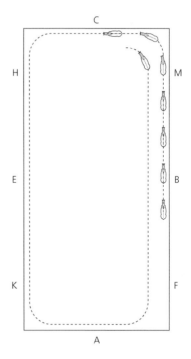

EXERCISE 147

4. CANTERING PAST THE INSIDE OF THE RIDE

RIDER LEVEL Intermediate and advanced.

AIMS AND BENEFITS

- Challenges the rider to maintain the canter past the ride.

EXERCISE 147

- The ride is in walk.

- Rear file halts to allow a gap to develop between them and the ride.

- The rider then overtakes the ride on the inside in trot.

- On reaching the front of the ride, the rider makes a canter transition in the next available corner, going large.

- Planning ahead, the rider maintains the canter past the inside of the ride.

- Taking up lead file position, the rider makes progressive transitions through trot to walk.

PROBLEMS

- The main area of weakness in this exercise is that most horses are used to coming into the rear of the ride and walking.
- In order for the rider to maintain the canter past the ride, the turn onto the inner track to pass the ride must be sufficiently early, so that the horse does not spy the rear of the ride and think that he is going to walk.

CIRCLES

1. CANTER WORK WITH THE RIDE DIVIDED ONTO TWO 20M CIRCLES

RIDER LEVEL Novice and intermediate.

AIMS AND BENEFITS
- Maintaining the shape and size of a 20m circle in canter.
- Rhythm.
- Balance.
- Confidence.

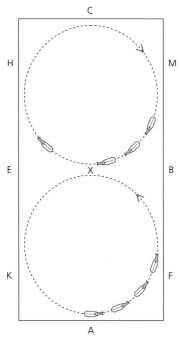

EXERCISES 148 and 149

EXERCISE 148

- One circle at a time, ask the ride to trot on their 20m circle, lead file in succession makes a transition to canter at a specific point, and maintains the canter to the rear of the ride on the circle. (With novice riders it is best to ask for canter between X and the boards, as the horse will begin the canter supported by the boards. This gives the riders time to organise themselves in the canter.)

- Depending on the ability of the ride, this may require help from the instructor.

- With intermediate groups, insist on accuracy of the transitions, using adequate preparation, with an accurate circle, maintaining balance and rhythm throughout.

PROBLEMS
- Lack of preparation for both upward and downward transitions.

EXERCISE 149 (INTERMEDIATE)

- As exercise 148, but ridden working both circles at the same time, depending on weather conditions and horses' temperaments.

PROBLEMS
- Horse falls in or out on the circle.

- Safety has priority. Before starting to work more than one rider in canter at the same time, you must be confident that all will maintain control.

EXERCISE 150

- Assuming that there are four on each circle, ask two riders to halt in the middle of the circle, or walk on a 10m circle, while the other two trot on their circle with half a circle distance between them.

- Either working one or both circles at a time, give the riders who are trotting the command to canter.

- The riders can be given a period of time to canter before returning to trot, e.g. one circle, returning to trot at the point at which the canter transition was made.

- Repeat once or twice more, enabling riders to make improvements, before swapping over and moving onto the riders who have been halted.

PROBLEMS

- Horses cantering tend to fall in to the middle of the circle towards the others in halt.

EXERCISE 151

- The above exercise can be ridden with emphasis on balance, rhythm, impulsion and shape of the circle, by asking the riders to count the number of strides on each half of the circle. The number should be the same.

PROBLEMS

- The number of strides is not the same. The reason for this must be assessed and corrected.

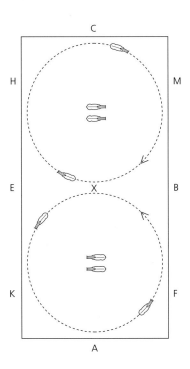

EXERCISES 150 and 151

2. CANTER ON A CIRCLE AT E/B

RIDER LEVEL Intermediate and advanced.

AIMS AND BENEFITS
- Cantering on a circle at E/B without the support of the boards.

EXERCISE 152

- With the ride in trot on a 20m circle at E/B, lead file in succession canter to the rear of the ride.

PROBLEMS
- Without the support of the boards, the rider will need to be in control of every footfall of the horse.

- Lack of co-ordination of the aids may lead to:
  – loss of shape of the circle,
  – loss of rhythm and balance,
  – horse breaking into trot.

EXERCISE 153

- With the ride in walk on a 20m circle at E/B, decrease the size of the circle to 15m.

- One rider at a time, leg yield out to 20m, make a transition to trot, and then canter.

- Canter one complete circle around the rest of the ride, return to trot and then walk as the rider's position in the ride is found.

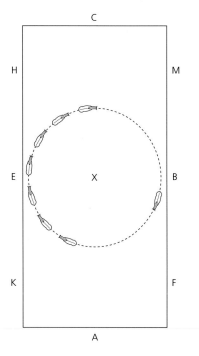

EXERCISE 152

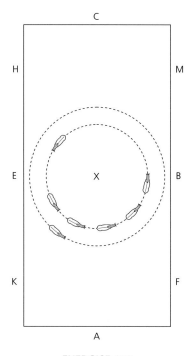

EXERCISE 153

PROBLEMS

- Riders will probably need to be strong with their aids to maintain the canter around the rest of the ride, as the horse is likely to wish to fall in and join the rest of the ride.

EXERCISE 154

- As exercise 153, but instead of cantering a circle around the ride, canter large, returning to the ride once a complete circuit of the school has been made.

PROBLEMS

- The horse may be reluctant to leave the rest of the ride.
- The horse is likely to try to break into trot as he passes the ride while going large.

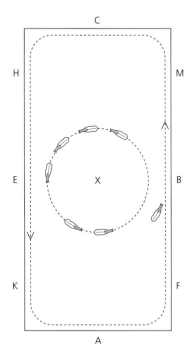

EXERCISE 154

- The rider will need to be aware and decisive in order to keep the horse between leg and hand and succeed with this exercise.

3. CANTER EXERCISES WITH THE RIDE DIVIDED ONTO TWO 15M CIRCLES

RIDER LEVEL Intermediate and advanced.

AIMS AND BENEFITS
- Independence.
- Rhythm.
- Balance.
- Accuracy.

EXERCISE 155

- Divide the ride onto two 20m circles at A/C, both on the same rein.

- Decrease the size of the circles to 15m.

- With the ride in walk, ask one rider at a time from each circle to leg yield out onto a 20m circle, at which point the rider makes a transition to trot.

- When they feel that they are prepared, the rider then makes a transition to canter.

- Canter one complete circle around the other riders, making a transition to trot at the point where the cantering started.

- Making a balanced transition to walk, the rider can return to their position on the 15m circle.

- Continue the exercise with the rest of the ride.

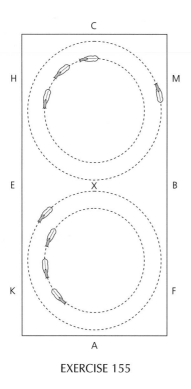

EXERCISE 155

• Riders can make a progressive transition through trot to walk and return to their place.

PROBLEMS

• While going large the canter becomes long and flat and the horse may break into trot if not kept between leg and hand.

• Loss of balance and rhythm in the canter.

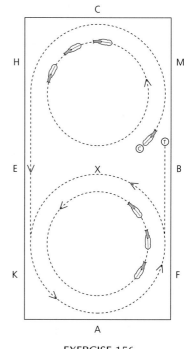

EXERCISE 156

Ⓣ = trot transition Ⓒ = canter transition

PROBLEMS

• The horse falls in on the circle towards the rest of the ride and loses the canter. The rider must take control of the situation and encourage the horse to listen by riding strongly with the aids.

EXERCISE 156

• As exercise 155, but this time as riders make the transition to canter, they go large.

• Circle 20m around the riders at the opposite end of the school.

• Riders continue large, returning to their own circle.

4. WALK TO CANTER FROM A 5M CIRCLE

RIDER LEVEL Advanced.

AIMS AND BENEFITS
- Accuracy.
- Preparation.
- Co-ordination of the aids.

EXERCISE 157

- With the ride divided onto two 20m circles, have two riders halted in the centre of each circle, with two walking on each circle, spread out evenly.

- The riders in walk will walk a 5m circle towards the halted riders.

- At the moment they rejoin the 20m circle, they will make a direct transition from walk to canter.

- Canter one complete circle, returning progressively to walk.

- The canter to walk transition can gradually be made more direct by spiralling the canter circle down to 12–15m, helping to collect the canter before asking for walk.

EXERCISE 158

- As exercise 157. To develop the exercise the riders could canter large to the circle at the opposite end of the school, before making their downward transitions. A 2–3m shallow loop could be introduced along the long side of the school.

PROBLEMS, Exercises 157 and 158
- The 5m circle helps to prepare the horses for the transition to canter. Ensure that it is ridden correctly, with energy.
- When the shallow loop is ridden, ensure that the bend remains over the lead leg.

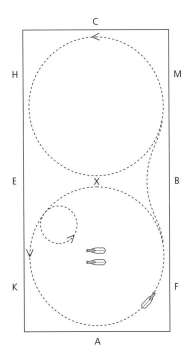

EXERCISES 157 and 158

5. CHANGE THE REIN AND CANTER A 20M CIRCLE

RIDER LEVEL Intermediate and advanced.

AIMS AND BENEFITS
- Sharpening the rider's preparation and aids.

EXERCISE 159

- Put the ride onto a 20m circle at A and decrease the size of the circle to 15m.

- One rider at a time, leg yield out to 20m and make a transition to trot.

- At X make a change of rein onto a 20m circle at C.

- Between X and the boards, make a transition to canter.

- Canter one complete circle before returning to trot.

- Change the rein on reaching X and return to the ride.

PROBLEMS
- The exercise requires maximum preparation to leg yield out, trot, change the rein and make a canter transition in a short space of time.

CENTRE LINE

See Chapter 5, School Figures, Exercises 79 and 80 (pages 53–54).

CANTER FROM LEG YIELDING IN TROT

See Chapter 8, Lateral Work, Exercises 121 and 122 (pages 76–77).

SHORTENING AND LENGTHENING

See Chapter 7, Lengthening and Shortening, Exercises 103, 104 and 105 (pages 66–67).

EXERCISE 159

11 DRESSAGE TESTS

The use of dressage tests within a lesson adds variety and interest. Often riders feel that they are a world away from competitive riders. By using a test within a lesson, it brings both of those worlds a little closer together. For those who aspire to own a horse one day, it will offer a very basic insight into what is expected when entering into a dressage competition. For interested riders, the instructor can talk about the competition day itself, from preparation and travelling, to warming up and riding the test itself. Explain the 'Collective Marks'.

If ridden individually, within a group, the lesson disappears into 5 minutes for each rider. It is therefore more beneficial to ride the test as a ride in walk and trot, using the canter exercise individually afterwards.

BEGINNER

An imaginative instructor can make up a very simple dressage test, which does not even include the centre line. Introduction to the work, repetition to improve it, and then a final ridden test, would be the structure of the lesson. If the instructor gives basic marks to each rider for the whole test, this will add variety to a lesson.

NOVICE

A very simple Preliminary test makes a wonderful challenge for the novice. Ride through any areas that may cause difficulties before putting it together as a ride in walk and trot – the canter work could be ridden in walk or trot. The canter exercise can be ridden individually afterwards. If the canter exercise is more demanding than this level would normally ride, then change it.

INTERMEDIATE

As for Novice, using a more difficult Preliminary test if suitable.

ADVANCED

As for Novice and Intermediate, using an easy Novice test. Be very strict on accuracy.

DRESSAGE TESTS FOR BEGINNERS

These are imaginary tests, made up for beginner riders as a simple exercise. When creating your own tests, try to keep them simple so that you can focus on achievable accuracy. Use leaders or not, as necessary.

TEST 1

With lead file halted at F on the right rein:

Whole ride walk	
A	20m circle
AKE	Walk
E	Working trot
A	Walk
KXM	Change the rein
C	20m circle
CHE	Walk
E	Working trot
EABC	Working trot
C	Walk
CHEK	Walk
K	Halt, salute

EXERCISE 160

- Ride the whole test (Test 1 or Test 2) in walk first, so that the riders become familiar with where they are going.

- Practise the areas of trot.

- Put the test together, in walk and trot.

- Children really enjoy saluting and, if you have parents watching, a round of applause will top off the lesson!

TEST 2

With lead file halted at M on the left rein:

Whole ride walk	
MCHE	Walk
E	Working trot
EA	Working trot
A	20m circle
AFBM	Working trot
M	Walk
MCH	Walk
HXF	Change the rein
FAKE	Walk
E	Working trot
EHC	Working trot
C	20m circle
CMBF	Working trot
F	Walk
FAKEH	Walk
H	Halt, salute

PROBLEMS

- Loss of shape of the circles – cones may help this.
- Horses break into walk, or cut corners – the instructor may need to support

DRESSAGE TEST FOR NOVICE RIDERS

EXERCISE 161

- Explain what a dressage test is and how it is marked, including the collective marks.

- Practise parts of the test before riding it all the way through:
  - centre line
  - 20m circles at E/B,
  - half 10m circles B-X-E,
  - medium walk and free walk on a long rein,
  - halt.

- Ride the test through once as a ride, riding the canter parts in walk or trot. This helps to familiarise riders with the test. Ensure that when reading, you allow sufficient time for the riders to prepare. You also need to be able to keep an eye on the riders so that you are able to offer individual help before they ride it a second time. It is not easy to read and watch the ride at the same time! It may help if you can memorise the test before the lesson so that you can pay more attention to the riders.

- Once you have spoken to the ride collectively and helped individuals as necessary, ride the test a second time. The second riding is normally a vast improvement on the first.

BRITISH DRESSAGE

PRELIMINARY 2002 — 4

Arena 20m x 40m
Approximate time 5 minutes

			Max. Marks
1.	A	Enter in working trot, proceed down centre line without halting	10
	C	Turn right	
2.	B	Circle right 20 metres diameter	10
	BFA	Working trot	
3.	A	Down centre line	10
	C	Turn left	
4.	E	Circle left 20 metres diameter	10
	EK	Working trot	
5.	between K & A	Working canter left	10
	AFB	Working canter	
6.	B	Circle left 20 metres diameter	10
7.	BCEK	Working canter	10
	K	Working trot	
8.	A	Medium walk	10
	B	Half circle left 10 metres diameter to X	
	X	Half circle right 10 metres diameter to E	

Prelim 4 continues overleaf

PROBLEMS

- Although this is an extremely valuable and enjoyable lesson, dressage tests are not designed to be ridden as a ride. As such, only the lead file will be making transitions at the correct letters. Explain to the rest of the ride that they have responsibility for making balanced transitions and concentrating on the quality of the pace and their positions. Rotating lead file, if time allows, may permit all riders to have the opportunity to ride the test accurately.
- Over- or under-shooting the centre line.
- School figures of inaccurate size and shape.
- Inaccurate use of letters when changing rein.

(Prelim 4 continued)			Max. Marks
9.	E between H & C CMB	Working trot Working canter right Working canter	10
10.	B	Circle right 20 metres diameter	10
11.	BAEH H	Working canter Working trot	10
12.	C MXK K A	Medium walk Change rein in a free walk on a long rein Medium walk Down centre line	10 x 2
13.	D G	Working trot Halt. Immobility. Salute	10
		Leave the arena in a free walk on a long rein where appropriate	
COLLECTIVE MARKS			
14.		Paces (freedom and regularity)	10 x 2
15.		Impulsion (desire to move foward, elasticity of the steps, suppleness of the back and engagement of the hindquarters)	10 x 2
16.		Submission (attention and confidence, harmony, lightness and ease of the movements, acceptance of the bridle and lightness of the forehand)	10 x 2
17.		Riders position and seat; correctness and effect of the aids	10 x 2
		Total	**220**

EXERCISE 162

- The canter exercise from a test can be ridden individually.

- Ride the exercise, lead file in succession, moving the rest of the ride around the school to keep out of their way.

- Taking the canter exercise from Preliminary 4 as the example:
  - with the ride in trot on the left rein,
  - the ride walks at K as lead file canters between K and A; lead file continues the canter exercise from the test;
  - the ride halts at F until the 20m circle at B has been completed, and then walks on;
  - the lead file will come into the rear of the ride once they have completed the exercise.

PROBLEMS

- Depending on experience, if the riders are not used to cantering a 20m circle at B or E, placing the circle at C instead should make the exercise easier. If the riders are not cantering circles, omit the circle, and simply canter large.

DRESSAGE TEST FOR INTERMEDIATE RIDERS

EXERCISE 163

- Practise parts of the test as a ride:
  - centre line,
  - half 10m circles and inclines,
  - turning from B to E,
  - medium walk and free walk on a long rein,
  - halt.

- As for novice riders, ride the test through twice as a ride. The areas of canter can be ridden in walk or trot. Offer advice after the first riding, and work to improve for the second riding.

- Be stricter with intermediate riders than novices regarding:
  - accuracy of the school figures and changes of rein,
  - correct bend,
  - rhythm and balance,
  - quality of the pace,
  - submission,
  - rider's position.

PROBLEMS

- Inaccuracy of the centre line.
- Loss of balance and rhythm, shape and size of school figures.
- Loss of balance during the turn from B to E – explain how to ride the corners.
- Insufficient difference shown between medium walk and free walk on a long rein.

BRITISH DRESSAGE

PRELIMINARY 2002 **10**

Arena 20m x 40m
Approximate time 4½ minutes

			Max. Marks
1.	A	Enter in working trot, proceed down centre line without halting	
	C	Turn right	10
2.	MBF	Working trot	
	FD	Half circle right 10 metres diameter, returning to the track at B	10
3.	B	Working trot	
	C	Circle left 20 metres diameter	10
4.	CHEK	Working trot	
	KD	Half circle left 10 metres diameter, returning to the track at E	10
5.	E	Working trot	
	C	Circle right 20 metres diameter	10
6.	CMB	Working trot	
	B	Turn right	
	E	Turn left	
	EKA	Working trot	10
7.	A	Working canter left	
	B	Circle left 20 metres diameter	10
8.	BMCH	Working canter	
	HXF	Change rein	
	F	Working trot	10
9.	A	Medium walk	
	KBM	Change rein in a free walk on a long rein	
	M	Medium walk	10 x 2

Prelim 10 continues overleaf

EXERCISE 164

- Canter the exercise from the test (Prelim 10) individually.

- Riders have probably rarely practised cantering across the diagonal. Explain how to maintain the correct bend and prepare for the transition to trot. Explain the importance of the riders' looking where they are going before they turn.

- Taking the canter exercise from Preliminary 10 as the example:
  - with the ride on the left rein, as the lead file canters at A, the rest of the ride halts at A;
  - this will mean that as the lead file changes the rein, they will need to trot a little before F and pass the ride on an inner track, before making a change of rein and returning to the rear of the ride.

PROBLEMS

- The most likely problem to occur will be when the rider canters across the diagonal: many riders will turn too much, and as they use the rein to try to return to the correct line, the horse may disunite.
- The horse breaks into trot early when ridden across the diagonal. The rider must try to keep the horse balanced between leg and hand.

(Prelim 10 continued)

			Max. Marks
10.	C E B	Working trot Turn left Turn right	10
11.	A E	Working canter right Circle right 20 metres diameter	10
12.	EHCM MXK K	Working canter Change rein Working trot	10
13.	A G	Down centre line Halt. Immobility. Salute	10

Leave the arena in a free walk on a long rein where appropriate

COLLECTIVE MARKS

14.		Paces (freedom and regularity)	10 x 2
15.		Impulsion (desire to move foward, elasticity of the steps, suppleness of the back and engagement of the hindquarters)	10 x 2
16.		Submission (attention and confidence, harmony, lightness and ease of the movements, acceptance of the bridle and lightness of the forehand)	10 x 2
17.		Riders position and seat; correctness and effect of the aids	10 x 2
		Total	**220**

DRESSAGE TEST FOR ADVANCED RIDERS

EXERCISE 165

- Practise parts of the test (Novice 21) as a ride:
  - centre line,
  - three-loop serpentine,
  - medium trot,
  - medium walk and free walk on a long rein.

- The horse must be in front of the leg for the rider to be able to make balanced transitions.

- Elements of the Novice test are closer together than the Preliminary, which means that riders must be thinking ahead and very prepared.

- Ride through the test twice, as for the other tests. Ride the canter work in walk or trot. Discuss the way it was ridden. Advanced riders may wish to spend a little time individually working to improve their horse's way of going before attempting the test again.

- Advanced riders should be aiming for:
  - accuracy,
  - the collectives: paces, impulsion, submission, position.

- Advanced riders should create a picture of harmony with their horse, through understanding, good communication and softness of the aids.

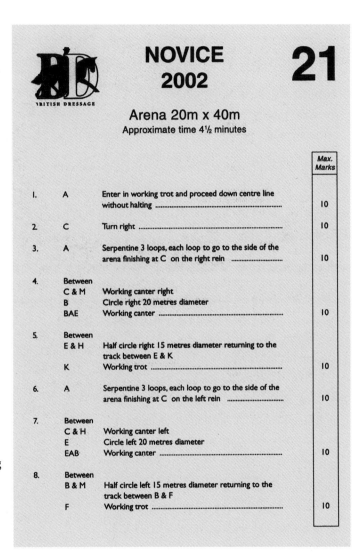

NOVICE 2002 **21**

BRITISH DRESSAGE

Arena 20m x 40m
Approximate time 4½ minutes

			Max. Marks
1.	A	Enter in working trot and proceed down centre line without halting	10
2.	C	Turn right	10
3.	A	Serpentine 3 loops, each loop to go to the side of the arena finishing at C on the right rein	10
4.	Between C & M B BAE	Working canter right Circle right 20 metres diameter Working canter	10
5.	Between E & H K	Half circle right 15 metres diameter returning to the track between E & K Working trot	10
6.	A	Serpentine 3 loops, each loop to go to the side of the arena finishing at C on the left rein	10
7.	Between C & H E EAB	Working canter left Circle left 20 metres diameter Working canter	10
8.	Between B & M F	Half circle left 15 metres diameter returning to the track between B & F Working trot	10

Novice 21 continues overleaf

PROBLEMS

- The horse's way of going is sacrificed for accuracy.
- Rhythm and balance may be lost at times during the school figures.
- Tension creeps into the rider's position through the effort of trying to ride the test well, and therefore the horse becomes tense.
- Medium trot strides are rushed and the horse falls on the forehand.

EXERCISE 166

- Ride the canter exercise individually.

- Taking the canter exercise from Novice 21 as the example:
  - with the ride on the right rein,
  - once the lead file canters between C and M, halt the ride at M;
  - once the lead file has cantered the 20m circle at B, walk the ride on, and halt again at F.
  - This means that once the lead file has made the transition to trot at K, they can come on the inside of the ride, change the rein and return to the rear of the ride.

- Time permitting, ride the canter exercise twice, the first time with the intention to join the track at K after the half 15m circle, at which point the transition to trot is ridden. The second time, ask the riders to join the track closer to E, which allows them to ride a short period of counter canter before their transition to trot at K. If the canter is ridden well, the riders may find that their transition to trot is actually more balanced

(Novice 21 continued)			Max. Marks
9.	FK KXM M	Working trot Change rein and show some medium trot strides Working trot	10
10.	C HXF F	Medium walk Change rein in a free walk on a long rein Medium walk	10 x 2
11.	A D G	Down centre line Working trot Halt. Immobility. Salute.	10
		Leave the arena in a free walk on a long rein where appropriate	
COLLECTIVE MARKS			
12.		Paces (freedom and regularity)	10 x 2
13.		Impulsion (desire to move foward, elasticity of steps, suppleness of the back and engagement of the hindquarters)	10 x 2
14.		Submission (attention and confidence, harmony, lightness and easeof the movements, acceptance of the bridle and lightness of the forehead)	10 x 2
15.		Rider's position and seat; correctness and effect of the aids.	10 x 2
		Total	200

following the counter canter.

PROBLEMS

- During the half 15m circle with incline, the canter may become tense, or the horse may break into trot for various reasons – rider tension, horse not between leg and hand, poorly ridden half 15m circle, insufficient use of the outside aids, loss of bend, lack of impulsion.

- Unless the canter is well ridden, the following transition to trot will be poor.

- Encourage riders to use the 20m circle to set the horse up for the more difficult movement.

12 DRILL RIDE WORK

Drill ride work can be very enjoyable and stimulating both to ride and teach. For riders it becomes a good test, putting into practice all that they have learned and adds the new dimension of teamwork to their riding. The instructor needs a good imagination and sense of humour!

Ensure that, when pairing horses, consideration is paid to which horses will be friendly together.

BEGINNER

Beginner riders may not suit drill ride work if they are very new to riding. If they are almost at novice level, then the easier exercises will add the new dimension of teamwork to their riding.

NOVICE

Ridden in walk and trot, the emphasis is not only on the rider's own quality of work, but also on teamwork and the pattern. Make the drill ride achievable – more simple than the work that they have been doing, as riding as a team is an underestimated challenge.

INTERMEDIATE

With the intermediate group that has practised drill riding before, the figures and movements ridden can afford to be more demanding than those of the novice group. Emphasis again is on the quality of the work from each individual, which will create a higher standard overall as a team.

ADVANCED

The advanced group should work towards maintaining the horses' correct way of going throughout. It may be possible to include periods of canter.

AIMS AND BENEFITS

- Riders can put into practice all that they have learned.
- Enjoyment.
- Teamwork.
- Variety.
- Co-ordination of the aids.
- Timing.

CENTRE LINE IN PAIRS

RIDER LEVEL Beginner and novice.

AIMS AND BENEFITS
- Introduction to drill riding.

EXERCISES 167–169

- Halt the ride on the centre line in pairs, facing C. (If there is an odd number, the instructor will need to stand in!)

EXERCISE 167

- Each pair in succession, walk on.

- Divide at the end of the school and, both partners of the pair keeping level, make a transition to halt at E/B for 5 seconds before continuing in walk.

- Turn up the centre line as a pair, halting at the rear of the ride.

EXERCISE 168

- Each pair in succession, walk on, divide at C.

- Make a transition to trot at M/H.

- Make a transition to walk at F/K.

- Turn up the centre line as a pair and halt at the rear of the ride.

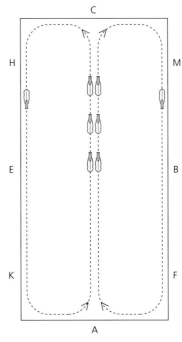

EXERCISES 167–169

EXERCISE 169

- Ask each pair to design their own sequence using the same format on the long sides of the school.

- The sequence should include halt, walk and trot.

PROBLEMS, Exercises 167–169
- Riding without consideration of partners.
- Lack of co-ordination of the aids required to achieve correct timing.
- Turning onto the centre line in pairs – explain that riders are not aiming for the centre line, but their side of it.

SIMPLE DRILL RIDE (EXERCISES 170–173)

RIDER LEVEL Novice.

AIMS AND BENEFITS
- A simple introduction to a drill ride with the whole group moving together.
- The exercises follow on from one another so that the drill ride is formed by riding them all in sequence.

EXERCISE 170

- Begin in walk with the ride in pairs on the centre line facing C.

- Divide at C.

- Turn up the centre line in pairs.

- Divide at C.

PROBLEMS

- Difficulty maintaining distance in the ride, and keeping level with partner.
- Over- or undershooting the centre line.

EXERCISE 171

- Ride a 20m circle at E/B with those on the right rein on the inside of those on the left rein.

PROBLEMS

- Those on the right, taking the inner track, will make up ground.

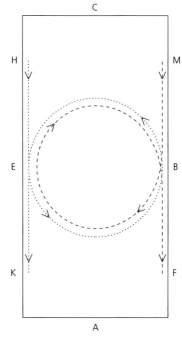

EXERCISE 171

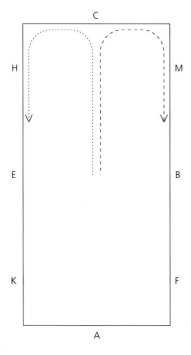

EXERCISE 170

EXERCISE 172

- Go large, passing at A and C, right rein on the inside.

PROBLEMS

- Again, the right rein will make up ground.

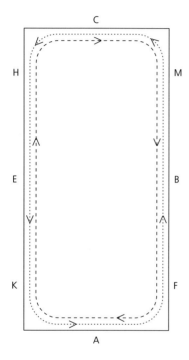

EXERCISE 172

EXERCISE 173

- Turn up the centre line in pairs.

- Halt when lead pair reaches G.

- Try parts or all of the drill ride in trot if it is polished in the walk.

PROBLEMS

- Centre line over- or undershot.
- Horses need to be lined up in their pairs for the halt.

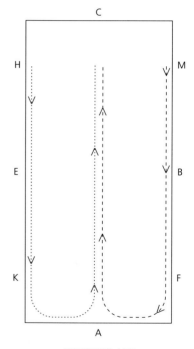

EXERCISE 173

MODERATE LEVEL DRILL RIDE (EXERCISES 174–177)

RIDER LEVEL Intermediate and advanced.

AIMS AND BENEFITS

- When the exercises are ridden in sequence they form the drill ride.
- A more challenging drill ride for more able riders.
- Accuracy.
- Parts for the advanced riders could be ridden in canter.

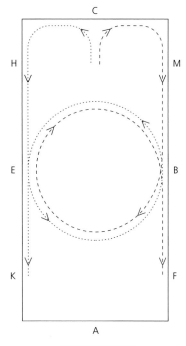

EXERCISE 174

EXERCISES 174–177

- Begin in walk for all riders to learn the sequence.

EXERCISE 174

- In pairs on the centre line, divide at C.

- Ride a 20m circle at E/B, right rein on the inside.

PROBLEMS

- Those on the right rein will tend to make up ground over those on the left rein.

EXERCISE 175

- Go large from E/B, passing at A.

- Both teams turn across the diagonals, FXH and KXM, crossing at X, alternate riders from each team in order.

- Pass at C.

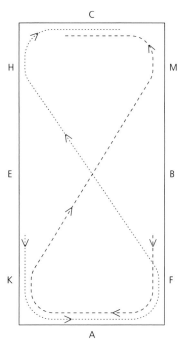

EXERCISE 175

PROBLEMS

- During the passing at A, the ride will need to ensure that they have one horse's distance between them, to have sufficient distance to be able to 'scissor' over X.

EXERCISE 176

- Along the next long side, both teams turn across the school individually so that both rides pass in between each other over the centre line.

- Both teams track towards A.

PROBLEMS

- To make this aesthetic, timing for the turn must be immaculate.

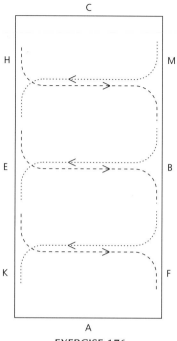

EXERCISE 176

EXERCISE 177

- Turn up the centre line in pairs.

- Halt as lead pair reaches G

PROBLEMS

- Ensure the riders halt in their pairs.
- The movements are close together. If necessary, offer more time to prepare by going large in between movements.
- Practise each movement separately before putting it together.

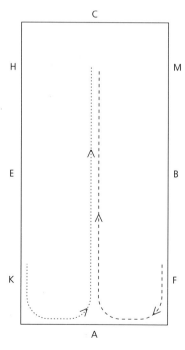

EXERCISE 177

13 EXERCISES USING POLES

The use of poles adds variety to lessons. They can be used as guides and markers to create transition boxes, and within balanced position or jumping lessons. In the two exercises outlined below, they help to improve the rider's awareness of rhythm and balance, and shortening and lengthening of the stride.

Pole work is very demanding of horses, and an instructor must monitor this carefully during lessons. There is also a small element of risk associated with horses treading on poles, which is why some instructors feel that the square poles are safer.

BEGINNER

The pole exercises outlined below are not suitable for the beginner rider.

NOVICE

Pole work can initially throw riders out of balance as the horse is more elevated in his stride over the pole. Aim to maintain the riders' positions throughout, to enable them to derive the most from the exercises. Riders should be made aware that they are to try to maintain the horse's balance and rhythm throughout.

INTERMEDIATE

Riders should aim for accuracy, balance and rhythm throughout, helping the horse to the best of their abilities. The rider's position should be more secure than that of the novice rider, and intermediates should therefore be more able to stay in balance with the horse.

ADVANCED

Advanced riders should look upon pole work as an opportunity to further develop their feel for riding the trot. Pole work should help to produce a more engaged and uphill feel for the rider.

AIMS AND BENEFITS

RIDER

- Variety.
- Enjoyment.
- Co-ordination.
- Accuracy.
- Feel.
- Position, especially in relation to balance.

HORSE

- Rhythm.
- Balance.
- Suppleness.
- Impulsion.
- Engagement.

THE FAN

RIDER LEVEL Novice, intermediate and advanced.

AIMS AND BENEFITS

- Correct assessment of the horse's length of stride.
- Riding a good line through the poles.
- Rhythm and balance.
- Shortening and lengthening.

EXERCISES 178 and 179

- Place three poles just inside the line of a 20m circle at A or C in the shape of a fan.

- The middle of the poles is set at a suitable distance for working trot for the average of the group.

- Towards the middle of the circle, the poles will be slightly narrower, towards the outer edge, slightly wider.

EXERCISE 178 (NOVICE)

- Ask each individual to decide whether he believes that his horse has a large, average or small natural working trot stride. This will determine where the riders aim for as they trot over the poles. Ensure that you confirm with each rider where he is aiming. For children, ask them to tell you whether their pony is small, medium or large within the group. (There may be slight variations within this as a small pony may have a large trot, and vice versa. This can be explained.)

- Once the riders know where they are aiming, ask the ride to trot on a 20m circle around the outside

of the poles. Ensure the trots are forward going.

- Lead file in succession rides his line on a curve over the poles. Once over the poles, he can trot a smaller circle to the rear of the ride and the next rider can take their turn.

- If the line over the poles was correct the rider should have felt no change in the length of stride.

- If the distance between the poles was too long, the rider should have felt the horse lengthen the stride to make the distance. This may have caused the rider to get left behind the movement and lean back.

- If the distance was too short, the rider should have felt the horse shorten the stride to make the distance. This may have caused the rider to be in front of the movement and lean forwards.

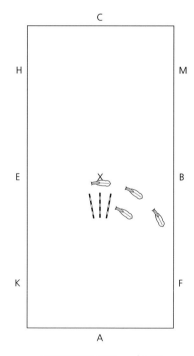

EXERCISES 178 and 179

- Repeat to improve.

PROBLEMS

- Insufficient energy in the trot, or insufficient leg over the poles and the horse therefore walks.
- Poor line over the poles.
- Loss of position which results in the rider not going with the movement.

EXERCISE 179 (INTERMEDIATE AND ADVANCED)

- This exercise can be ridden in ride or open order for the more able riders. If they are to work in open order:

  – limit the number of times that they are to go over the poles,

  – ensure that they do not follow too closely behind another horse so that if a pole is knocked it can be replaced,

  – make them aware that if a pole is knocked, no one is to ride over the poles until it has been replaced.

- Good intermediates and advanced riders can work to shorten and lengthen the stride over the poles. This will require them to take another line, so that they are aiming for the wider or narrower ends.

- Ask the riders to approach the poles in their shortened or lengthened trots.

PROBLEMS

- An over- or under-estimated change in length of stride.

THE CLOCK

RIDER LEVEL Novice, intermediate and advanced.

AIMS AND BENEFITS

- Awareness of balance and rhythm.

EXERCISE 180

- Place a pole at each quarter of a 20m circle, on a slightly inner track so that the ride can safely move around the poles on the circle.

- With the ride in an active trot on the 20m circle, lead file in succession trot a 15–18m circle over the poles, counting the number of steps in between the poles. The number should be the same in each quarter.

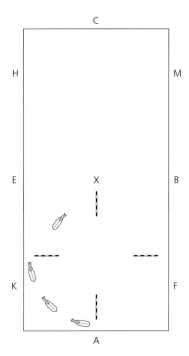

EXERCISE 180

- For good intermediate and advanced groups, the rider can then work to shorten and lengthen the stride within the exercise.

PROBLEMS

- The riders focus on riding to the poles rather than riding the shape of the circle. As a result the shape of the circle is lost, and therefore also the balance and rhythm.
- Horse loses impulsion due to the rider using insufficient leg.
- Loss of rider balance, and therefore position.

These two exercises could be ridden in the same lesson by placing the clock at one end of the school, and the fan at the other.

14 GAMES AND OBSTACLE COURSES

Games and obstacle courses do not need to be reserved for children. A good instructor can encourage the enjoyment of games to span the generations. If a structured plan is followed weekly during the course of a year, Christmas is a lovely time to play games, for all involved. An instructor may also find that there are certain times of the school year when children lack energy, such as towards the end of each school term. At these times, playing games in the lesson may inspire those who would otherwise lose concentration.

BEGINNER
The beginner rider will require very basic games that are achievable. Encouraging lots of noise in the form of cheering will create a great atmosphere for the simplest game.

NOVICE, INTERMEDIATE AND ADVANCED
With every game it is possible to make it as simple or as complicated as you like. Each game can be adjusted according to the rider level.

IMPORTANT NOTE
Most people are competitive. For this reason, occasionally riders throw caution to the wind during games, and this can lead to potentially dangerous situations. When explaining the rules of the game, encourage safety, without dampening spirits.

CHILDREN'S GAMES

TRAFFIC LIGHTS

With the ride going large in open or semi-open order, play the 'Traffic Lights' game:

RED – STOP

YELLOW – WALK

GREEN – TROT

PURPLE – CANTER (for advanced groups)

PINK – TURN A SMALL CIRCLE

The last one to fulfil the command is 'out' and comes to stand in the middle of the school. It is always worth having a couple of practice runs first, so that the one who is 'out' first feels that they have participated in the game initially.

SIMON SAYS

Every child knows this game, and therefore there is little explanation needed before the game can start. This is a good game to play with tiny tots and beginners as it helps to build confidence and can teach them parts of the horse and tack.

Placing both reins into one hand, (ensure that the outside rein is shorter), Simon Says touch your:

- Head.
- Shoulder.
- Tummy.
- Knee.
- Toe.
- Saddle.
- Parts of the saddle.
- Reins.
- Ears of the horse.
- Tail of the horse.
- Other parts of the horse within reach.

To make it a little more difficult, use the terms inside and outside, to encourage familiarity with these terms and to aid the understanding of their use when teaching. For example, 'Simon Says touch your outside knee'.

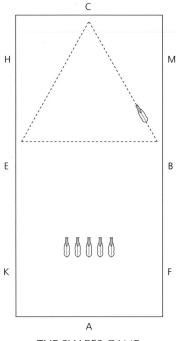

THE SHAPES GAME

THE SHAPES GAME

With the ride halted at one end of the school, facing the opposite end, each rider in turn walks or trots a shape at the free end of the school. The rest of the ride can guess the shape. (The instructor needs to have plenty of easy shapes in mind for any rider who struggles to think of one.)

TEAM GAMES FOR ADULTS AND CHILDREN

Place five cones along the three-quarter line on both sides of the school and divide the ride into two evenly matched teams. Ask the teams to create a name for themselves, and encourage cheering of the team name, or individual name as each rider races. Saying something like, 'the louder you cheer, the faster your ponies will go', usually animates the riders. Also, giving points for the team who cheers the loudest for each race will help to get the noise levels up. It is the cheering that really makes or breaks games, as the cheering creates the atmosphere.

RACE VARIETIES

- Walk up and back, weaving in and out of the cones.

- Trot straight up, walk weave back.

- Trot up and back, weaving.

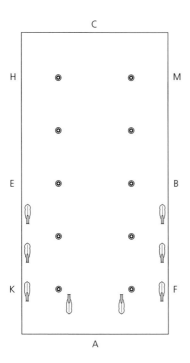

CONES SET OUT FOR RACES

OBSTACLE COURSES FOR CHILDREN AND ADULTS

These can be ridden as individual or as team courses, timed or with points allocated. The lesson can be structured so that each element of the obstacle course is practised before putting it together.

Elements that could be included:

- Cones to weave through.
- A jump.
- Dismount and lead.
- Pick up and drop.
- A halt box.
- Around the world (a leader would be needed to hold the pony).

- Trot weave up, pick up an object such as a sponge which has been placed in a suitable position, trot back and drop the object into a bucket.

- Give each rider a piece of carrot which they can drop into a bucket at the end of the cones.

- As fast as you can race, weaving or not.

To make the races more difficult:

- If the riders miss the bucket, they need to dismount and retrieve the object themselves.

- Weave in and out of the cones with the reins in one hand.

- Give each team a short whip as a baton, which must be swapped between riders before their turn.

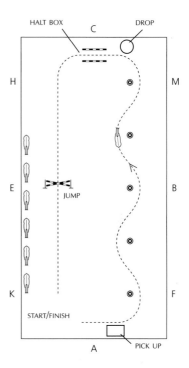

EXAMPLE OBSTACLE COURSE

ALSO AVAILABLE

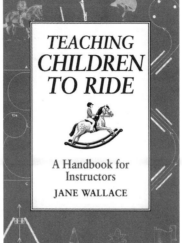

An enormously popular 'cookbook' of ideas and specimen exercises, compiled particularly for trainee instructors; also very useful for more experienced instructors and for riders schooling their own horses or ponies.

For everyone teaching 4–12-year-olds at riding schools, clubs or at home. Contains advice, exercises, lesson plans, games and teaching tips designed to provide variety and sound instruction, plus a fund of innovative ideas for making learning to ride an enjoyable, worthwhile and satisfying experience, even for the very young.

A collection of exercises, on the flat and over fences, specifically designed for use in training more experienced riders and horses, whether in groups or as individuals, or schooling at home.

Available from good bookshops and saddlers, or direct from
Kenilworth Press, an imprint of Quiller Publishing Ltd, Wykey House, Wykey,
Shrewsbury, SY4 1JA tel: 01939 261616 fax: 01939 261606 or visit the website:
www.kenilworthpress.co.uk to order on-line